Rapid Eye Technology

by Ranae Johnson, DCH, RET

with Joseph Bennette

Other Books by Ranae Johnson
Winter's Flower

With Joseph Bennette
Self-Discovery Processing With Rapid Eye Technology

Rapid Eye Technology

by Ranae Johnson, DCH, RET

with Joseph Bennette

PUBLISHED IN THE UNITED STATES BY RAINTREE PRESS, SALEM, OR.

This book is dedicated to all those who have been with me on my journey, especially to my husband, Joseph, who has been by my side, my children for their support, and all those who are working toward the healing of the planet.

Acknowledgments

Deep love and appreciation:

To my son, Kelton, who, through his autism, was my teacher.

To my wonderful husband, Joseph, for his love, patience and support. To my beautiful children, grandchildren and family who have supported and been there for me.

For the many things we learned from clients and RET technicians.

To my talented team of researchers and writers who contributed to this book:

Joseph Bennette   Kevin Beckstrom

Carol Bennette   Lynelle Beckstrom

Sonja Lorrigan Redford

And most of all, to God, for the inspiration to put the model of RET together.

Table of Contents

Table of Contents (cont'd)

Introduction

Carl Jung first introduced "synchroneity" as *the simultaneous occurrence of two meaningfully but not causally connected events. Collaboration does exist between people and events, and that collaboration seems to always be operating in the universe. "* He goes on to state *"we have an intelligence that is perfect, it has deep meaning and purpose, and operates in a synchronized fashion."*

Jung further stated: *"At the very moment when we are struggling to sustain a sense of personal autonomy, we also get caught up in vital forces that are much larger than ourselves. So that while we may be the protagonists of our own lives, we are the extras or spear carriers in some larger drama."*

All of us have had things happen that seem totally out of character and we later come to understand why. This mind-illuminating experience is called a connection, an "a-ha", or "hook-up". Connections happen even if we can't see them or understand them. Once we understand that everything is connected in some way, synchronism becomes more believable. Once we've accepted that thought could possibly exist out-side of us, then we are on our way to understanding synchronism (see *"You'll See It When You Believe It,"* Dyer).

The hook-up between seemingly unconnected events is really the hook-up of thought, the essence of our universe. It is a vibrating energy that we cannot see or define.

1

As I came to understand this principle, I could see the synchronicity that had occurred in my life. Throughout my life, I had to deal with the death of many people who were close to me. Those experiences in my life gave me pieces to a puzzle that I was able to use with the healing of my autistic son, Kelton. It also contributed to the Rapid Eye Technology model I developed. The puzzle pieces of life fit together perfectly and the old belief that unexplained coincidences occur for no reason gradually became a belief of the past.

Each event in a person's life leads to the next event. Each lesson is preceded by the exact set of lessons which prepared that person to be able to move along a continuum of learning. When a lesson is presented and is not learned, another series of experiences will take the person to an arena where they can re-create the lesson at a different level. This process will continue to be repeated until the lesson is learned.

Dr. Wayne Dyer wrote, *"The universe is complete and perfect. There can be no mistakes. Nothing is random. The entire 'onesong' is exquisitely synchronized."*

Looking back, I know that synchronism connected the very fabric of every experience in my life. Some years back, my husband Joseph and I were in the home building profession. We had the inspiration to purchase six acres of land close to our home in Salem, Oregon. We looked at the swampy pasture land filled with blackberry bushes and wondered if we had misunderstood.

The feeling was quite definite about the purchase, and it persisted. We chose to listen and bought the parcel of land, although we still weren't quite certain why.

Over the next six years we continued to follow the direction of our intuition. We planted trees, cleared the land and built a two story building on the property. The building was very large and it just sat there. At the time we didn't have a use for it. We continued to work on the land, waiting to discover its purpose.

Then, suddenly, financial problems hit us hard. It was as if all distractions in our lives were being removed. We relocated to our piece of land. We then received the instruction from the spirit to open *The Center for Self Discovery*. Since that time we have realized that it is a perfect place for healing to occur. We have water on our land, when our neighbors do not. We have planted blueberries on the land to earn money to speed the work of healing. Many things, such as carpeting and furniture, just come to us from other people, all without us asking anyone but the universe for it.

We now totally believe we're not in charge. We have learned to get in the flow and allow the universe to bring to us what we need to accomplish our healing work.

We have developed the Rapid Eye Technology process now teach it to others. We only play a small part, however, in the great healing work taking place in many dimensions of life.

Dr. Dyer's book *Real Magic* also states: *"The plan of nature seems to be nothing more than a slow and steady unfoldment of consciousness... . We can choose to function at a lower level of awareness and simply exist, caring for our possessions, eating, drinking, sleeping and managing in the world as pawns of the elements, or we can soar to new and higher levels of awareness allowing ourselves to transcend our environment and literally create a world of our own—a world of real magic. "*

Each of us is "at choice" in our lives whether we recognize it or not! When we realize we are completely responsible for the choices which create our lives, we are then in a position to change the things we don't like and we can ultimately set into motion a different reality. By making different choices, we are accessing an alternative synchronicity which will align with another reality. You may remember seeing this portrayed in the recent movie "Ground Hog Day" where the main character kept doing it over and over til he got it "right"!

Synchronicity is happening whether or not we are aware of it. Rapid Eye Technology assists you in becoming aware of the responsibility you have for creating the life you want. It opens your eyes to the fact that *you are accountable for the choices you make!* As you contemplate this statement, it is so important to understand that the only way you can have the power to change your life is to recognize it is something you created yourself. If you see yourself only as a "victim of circumstances" you are powerless to change anything. You will always be waiting around for somebody else to "fix" your life!

The first section of this book tells you a little about how the RET model was originated. You will learn about how Rapid Eye Technology works. We release traumatic memories on many levels of consciousness and bring many different forms of healing together in concert to create what we believe is a profound healing model.

Part Two investigates the second half of RET which deals with the important work of reframing the traumatic memories through learning in depth skills contained in the Seven Principles of Growth . Learning new living skills constitutes the cognitive work each client must do to enable them to collapse old belief systems which created the compulsive behaviors they experience every day. Not only are you introduced to new thinking patterns, but you will understand why knowing isn't enough. Releasing old habits and addictions promises a better chance of not recreating the pain in a different form.

The third part of this book provides an understanding of how you can be trained as a certified Rapid Eye Technician, qualified to assist in the healing of others. You learn the important difference between being a technician, (one who assists a person in discovering his/her own healing) and a counselor (who offers diagnoses and gives advice).

You also get a look at the vision of this "Self Discovery

Process", or Rapid Eye Technology. It invites you to clear your own emotional toxins and extend yourself to assist others in becoming empowered to find joy and peace, and unconditional love for self and others. You will gain an awareness of what your full potential is once you have "unzipped" the garment of traumatic memories and stepped into the light of Unconditional Love.

And finally, **the fourth part of this book focuses on** the extensive technical research which will give the reader a better understanding of the interconnectedness of all our experiences on the physical, emotional and mental levels. You will gain a respect for the miracle our body is. You will be excited to learn how intelligent every molecule of your body is...how it was designed to correct any condition which is "out of balance" in order to restore you to complete health if you will only seek to understand the signals it is giving you. You may gain a profound sense of respect for the importance of working with your body rather than against it. It is truly our greatest renewable resource!

This research into *why* RET works includes case studies which will give you insight into *how* Rapid Eye Technology has helped clients from every walk of life be able to be free of energy-draining, even life-threatening, compulsive behaviors. In these studies, you will recognize unhealthy patterns that may be apparent in yourself or your loved ones.

Hopefully, you will have a desire to seek out a certified RET technician to learn how you or your loved ones can benefit from this new technology.

You'll come to understand how healing through RET caused one client to exclaim, *"You have given me back my life!"*

THE WEAVERS

Quietly, just beneath the surface of awareness,
Those who love us in the way of oneness
Gently, persistently,
Weave all the tattered loose ends of
Experience into a beautiful ethereal
Fabric that will be viewed only from
Beyond time and space.

When we grasp the perception of
Simple peace, we are able to discern
The wisdom which releases our will
And we surrender to the work of
The Weavers.

Their work of love prepares us to
Pass the limits of this restricted
Jurisdiction where we flex our
Energy and strike the delicate balance
Between our strength and
Our vulnerability.

Precious cloth, value high.
This pattern requires just the right measure.
A shudder rips through as the fabric is torn.

Do not fear, have faith my child.
These are the skilled hands which fashion
The raiment for Sons and Daughters of Light.

Sonja Lorrigan Redford

Part One

Rapid Eye Technology - Processing The Pain

Ranae's History

Someone once told me that we all have our place in the world and all we have to do is relax into it. As a young struggling mother surrounded by scattered toys and cookie crumbs, I had no idea what that meant! In those days, I believed I had to *make* things happen. I believed in struggle! The turmoil I generated from my belief system was amazing, and it was all part of my growth cycle. It would be many years and trials later before I would even begin to understand how to surrender my beliefs for higher transformative experiences.

At first it was important to learn within a world of familiar values. Sometimes my growth looked and felt dangerous. Many of my lessons consisted of a lot of pain. Looking back, I realize the pain gave me complexity and I gained depth of character and a much greater perspective of life. Overcoming the pain required an opening to love's many forms. At first the "it's not my fault" cycle repeated itself over and over again. I didn't realize all learning is based on remembering, or accepting, the learning value of one's own mistakes. Perhaps the greatest learning experiences require taking the biggest risks, making the biggest mistakes! Then we attain the more important successes.

As children grow and experience life, each situation presents them with mini-messages revealing what life is about.

These mini-messages, known as "life scripts", can become stretched and distorted in a way that can affect life as an adult and how that adult not only perceives but processes the world. These slanted beliefs can become traumatic memories and can constrict the possibilities out of life.

I was born the oldest girl in a family of fourteen children. We were raised on a windy, dusty farm in the southwest corner of Wyoming, near the Utah border. The area was filled with lots of sage brush and rattlesnakes. I never learned to appreciate any of them!

As I grew up, seven of my brothers and sisters died. Later, two successive husbands and both parents passed on. My life script became "everyone I love leaves me."

The farm we lived on was not big enough to support a large family. I remember when I was about four years old, my mother convinced my father to lease our farm and move to the city. The farm had sheltered us during the depression and it was a very big risk to leave what my father felt was security. My memories were of excitement, but I sensed his uncertainty as we traveled to the city.

At first it was wonderful being in a new environment living a life totally different from the one I had experienced. As the year progressed, I watched my father become increasingly sad. We all missed the farm animals and the freedom of roaming the hills. The fresh, clean Wyoming air was becoming a distant memory. We would no longer rise early and gaze out over newly-plowed fields or watch the deer come for water. We missed the familiar smells and the color of harvest.

It seemed to me my father always returned to the familiar rather than risk new growth. Despite my father's best efforts, we remained in poverty. A year and a half later we returned to the farm.

Since my father's choices to stay with the familiar had not

worked, this experience taught me to do just the opposite. Another of my messages became: "If life is a risk anyway, it's better to risk something unfamiliar than risk the poverty of stagnation."

My pattern eventually led to venturing out and taking risks. The journey has been sometimes painful, but the reward was always growth.

When I was five and a half years old, my younger sister, Gaylene, burned to death while playing with matches. I had been very close to her and it felt like I had lost my own baby. The loss was so great that the whole family grieved for many years.

After Gaylene's death, it was discovered I had rickets, a debilitating disease caused by malnutrition. For a time I was sent off to stay with my mother's sister in the city. Our family was separated from each other for a number of months. The loss of my whole family at that age was devastating to me. I withdrew into myself and began to view the world as a hostile place.

Losing Gaylene was to me the most painful of the deaths of my siblings. It took a lot of soul searching for many years to understand why and how this pain would serve me.

My life continued mirroring and reflecting my fear thoughts of death as I seemed to attract other people into my life who either died or left. At nineteen I became a widow after my husband was killed in an accident. I was left as a single mother with two small children.

My father became more involved in my life after my husband's death. Our relationship deepened over the next couple of years as I struggled as a single mother. I never imagined my father would die when I was only twenty-one years old. I remarked one day about how I was really just getting to know my father on a different level. The next day he died! His death changed the life of each member of our family.

With his death I searched more deeply within myself. I found a tremendous source of inspiration from the Spirit and gained the energy to go on. When the grieving was complete, I returned to the outside world a very different person. Each time I withdrew into my silent world I gradually became acquainted with the experience of someone leaving. The emotional and mental grieving created a contraction of energy. Contraction occurred when I wasn't loving myself.

I learned my spirit resides partially in time and partially in eternity. As I came to understand this, I attended to my spirit's needs in many ordinary ways. Ordinary events have a way of walking us through a soul journey when we least expect it. As my personal healing occurred, I noticed a shift in my energy. The more I released sorrow, the more I was able to love myself, the higher my vibrational level (life-force energy) became. Everything went so much better when I could get away from negative thinking.

During those years impulses of sadness stirred me to the core of my being. I was living out a very complex story, often unconsciously. I gradually began to replace the deep depression and sadness with a flicker of understanding which allowed me to appreciate the process. I began unraveling the shifting experiences to find the meaning hidden within each one. Finally, a deep sense of gratitude replaced confusion.

When I was twenty-five, my second husband and I were blessed with our fourth child, Kelton. I had repeatedly prayed I would not lose children to death like my parents had. What I hadn't realized was that there are things much worse than death. Just as I decided I'd had my share of lessons, we discovered Kelton was autistic. It seemed so unfair!

As I looked deep into my feelings, I could hear my very being crying out, "No way!"

CHOOSE AGAIN

(The burden of experience is great.
So many to nurture and protect.
Oh, don't they see my strength is spent...
Is there no pause for rest?)

Child of love, heart of tenderness,
Yours is the fragile gift of guardianship.
When did you decide to choose this task?

How well I remember your trademark...
Eyes welled with tears,
Mouth tensed into a tight smile
That is strong as steel;
Holding back the flood of feelings
You deny yourself to express.

Fascinating combination of rigid restraint
And absolute raw emotion!
(Who will win this tug-of-war?
Frightened child...or...Daughter of Light?)

Elect daughter,
Explorer of this dispensation,
How long before you remember
Your birthright...your right to BE...free!

It is only the illusion
that counterfeits.

Choose again.

Sonja Lorrigan Redford

For years the great need to heal myself became subordinate to my stewardship to find a way to heal my child. Since science had not yet solved the riddle of autism, all I knew was my child was enslaved by some unknown silent darkness! From within my own pain, I seemed to sense the depth of love necessary to sustain him as we spent years working through his healing process.

Through my son's condition came a different understanding of life than I'd had before. Again I was to become aware of an important principle. It was a gift of learning that could only come to me through pain!

Mothering is a complex way to learn. It is not a simple matter of taking care of the immediate needs of another. There are many other ingredients. It is the recognition that each child has a special character and quality of spirit.

I was about to learn about spiritual mothering or "connection." I would learn to look at my son from a whole plan. His condition didn't make any sense on the physical level. Thoughts of unworthiness, fear, anger and guilt stopped the flow of inspiration and paralyzed my thinking. Fear threw me into disorder. Fear of the unknown, the unseen, and the unheard restructured me on all levels and caused feelings of separateness, misunderstanding and loss of self-worth.

With Kelton, I experienced a walk into darkness that enlarged both our souls. I learned spiritual mothering is only concerned with the walk of the soul. Evidently the way Kelton and I chose to learn was through pain.

I was to understand that trust is necessary to the broader picture. It took a great deal of faith because I had no idea what the picture was. The only thing I could do was to believe— have faith—that there is a plan and at some time that plan would be revealed to me. Until then, I learned to be grateful for each moment that strengthened the connection between us.

I know now an invisible connection always existed between my children and me. I always knew when my children needed me. With Kelton, the connection I developed went far beyond this relationship. If I was to help him heal, this connection had to be refined. I had to put my own suffering aside and learn to be *in the moment* for Kelton.

Later, not only to help my son, but also to create a model of therapy that helps others, I was motivated to search for and discover the uniqueness inside me. The discoveries I made eventually evolved into the model that became Rapid Eye Technology (RET). Thus I was truly able to serve others from my pain.

This refinement took some time to accomplish. I gradually learned to spend my time dwelling on what "might be" rather than what "might have been", —allowing my mind to slip into the *silent realm of infinite possibilities!*

As I became more skilled, I grasped the idea of *connection*. With each new obstacle came the understanding that it was a blessing.

My journey with life has provided me the opportunity to stop projecting blame. As I had once invited blame into my life, I now began to understand the importance of forgiveness. Forgiveness of God, myself, family, doctors, my husbands who died or left, and my son. I was able to step outside myself through forgiveness.

Things are hardly ever as bad as they appear to be, and I discovered much more character being built out of the trials and errors of daily life. My inventiveness had to enlarge as I experienced the shadows I found as I voyaged through each lesson. All my successes were built on the rubble of my past failures. There was always a spark of creativity shrouded in every veil of darkness.

My task then was to allow myself to get past fear and

despair, and quietly replace it with forgiveness. Failure seemed to bring regret. That belief furnished me with many reasons to get stuck in feelings of helplessness, missed chances, sadness, and a chance to live in the gray area that Thomas Moore calls "neither victory nor defeat".

In order for me to create conditions of growth, I knew I had to risk going beyond all my self-imposed boundaries and limitations.

Fortunately, most of my adversity did not take on the mantle of tragedy for very long. Life simply had to go on! I accepted there was a bigger picture. In this acceptance, I was nourished and comforted and the regrets began to retreat.

I once read a formula for growth: "It is the potential within me that equals the resistance I come up with, sent out through thought, then multiplied by the thoughts I let in from the world."

Of course, I would not learn this or even begin to understand it until the pain passed and my healing was more complete.

A seed has the potential of a tree; in order for the tree to form deep roots it must not have too much water or the roots become dependent on the water. If that happens, they never seek for any moisture on their own.

The resistance is the lack of water and the strong wind that comes into the life of the tree. The tree sends out thoughts continually to its branches, twigs and leaves. It also gains information from within and without. It senses winter is coming. The effect of this sensing is that the leaves drop and the tree becomes dormant, or "goes within" to regroup. Vast wisdom is stored in the rings of the tree and serves as growth. Growth comes to each of us in different ways.

GROWTH

The time-worn frame stands silhouetted against a
Fog-drenched early-morning horizon.
Barren, calloused arms reaching out,
For whom? For what?

How majestic the old apple tree stands with each limb and twig
Exposed to the view of casual passersby.
Never mind there is no shield from the glance of hasty judgment...
Eyes that recognize only obvious beauty.

Indeed, the old tree has been through this drama many times before.
Winter sap gently oozing to seal fresh cuts left by the
Snip, snip snip of the pruner's blade.

Such a necessary task, sending vigor back down to the roots,
Promising the strength needed for the advancing season of growth.

With the warmth of spring will come the delicate blossoms
Followed by tender, almost translucent leaves.
Activity abounds as the bees swarm in the May sunshine,
Transporting precious pollen, assuring fruition.

Soon there will be a need to thin the clusters of tiny apples,
Allowing strength to focus on the growth of
Those few chosen to remain.
Branches overburdened with abundance will need
Careful support to prevent injury to the fruiting wood.

Finally comes the harvest, a bounteous yield which
nourishes all who will partake.
Then follows another season of slumber to prepare for
the ongoing process...

How similar are the cycles of her journey.
So many different passersby,
Judging value which escapes their understanding.

Unshed tears bathe the fresh cuts of the Master Pruner.
But, in silence, she firms her jaw, squares her shoulders and
Strengthens her faith.

Soon the nakedness of her inner framework is
Clothed in the fragile blossoms of anticipation.
Activity abounds with the pollination of new ideas.

As she manifests the abundance of her inner vision,
She knows there will be a glorious harvest,
Followed by yet another season of growth..

Sonja Lorrigan Redford

Moving into a more loving place, I attracted many teachers and books. For me, the most profound class I took was called "A Course in Miracles." This is a course in learning to love unconditionally. I found new friends who were working on growth through loving others. I was introduced to ideas I hadn't thought of before. It wasn't so much that I changed my belief system, as I began to look at my beliefs from a different perspective.

After taking this training, I began developing my own class on *The Seven Principles*, which eventually attracted and helped many people.

In working through my own issues I found the best way to learn was to teach. As I began to teach the principles that had changed my life, I found they were changing the lives of others as well.

Gradually I came to understand that the deaths in my family prepared me for a much greater journey. In my case (and, I think, in most people's case), it is the pain that drives a person to heal and begin the journey within. My great inner desire to discover new truth moved me to imagine and visualize with exceptional range and depth. This was a process that took many years.

For a long time, life to me was just survival. The fact that I survived death, grief, anger, poverty and the many trials of my own married life was a great gift to me. I came to understand that life was not going to change, so I would simply have to change how I perceived it! When I felt despair and discouragement, I began to get in touch with my spirit, the part of me that resides in eternity (I refer to this as my "higher self"). I learned to see the deeper meaning hidden within each experience.

I began to realize it was important for me to "ask" my higher self for the learning I desired to have revealed. More than anything else, I desired to be healed, to be whole, to be restored to the person I really am! Once I made the inner commitment to be healed, my unhealed places had no choice but to come to my conscious awareness where I could process them.

Gradually, people were drawn into my life who would play the necessary roles which would facilitate my healing process. All my subconsciously-crafted blocks to keep love out began to reveal themselves to my conscious awareness. I learned to release fear! I learned to love! I learned to choose again!

Life is a cycling of events, all designed to teach unconditional love of self and others. When learning occurs, it is a life-changing experience, propelling us onward and upward toward higher consciousness. We go in one direction until one of two things happens: we refuse to learn the lesson in this arena and we are allowed to move to another experience where the lesson is repeated at another level, or the lesson is learned and we are sent in another direction pursuing yet another lesson..

TURNING THE TIDE

How do you detect the presence of pain
If pain is all you've ever known?
When pain is your constant companion
you never consider "how you feel."

You naturally assume it is the manner in which all feel.
Everything around you is filtered through this veil
And you adjust to the condition.
It is "normal" for you.

Within each of us is a clock,
Some mysterious something that knows
When we are ready for change.
Some power from within which turns the tide.

One day... almost imperceptively
Something deep within begins to stir.
You have stepped across the threshold
Of your willingness to tolerate pain.

There is no monument which marks this passageway.
But once you have stepped through that doorway
You will never be the same.
You have begun to heal.

*****

The rhythmic lapping of the waves
Gently lulls me into a quiet solitude.
Always moving, always changing.
Each new tide brings with it a washing... a cleansing
Of the life which teams beneath the surface.

Just like clockwork, oblivious to external influences
Since the beginning of time:
The tide comes in,
It turns,
The tide goes out,
It turns....

The turning of the tide teaches a lesson
To those who seek to learn:
The only constant condition.... is change.

Sonja Lorrigan Redford

Rapid Eye Technology

In this section, I will present the technical explanation on the physical, emotional and mental levels of Rapid Eye Technology (RET) as we have developed it at the Center for Self Discovery. The procedure is revolutionary and evolving. It represents extensive research and is the result of obedience to inspiration. When we are healed on these levels, we are awakened to our spiritual level, which is always there.

Treatment with Rapid Eye Technology is divided into two components, and is quite different from more traditional psycho dynamic therapies. These two parts work together to bring the client into a state of wellness.

One part is the actual RET sessions wherein the technician assists the client to get in touch with the emotions which have been "trapped" inside and never expressed. Then, through the process of RET, the client is able to release this distorted energy and be restored to a healthier state.

The other part is cognitive work. It is the active learning and practicing of effective living skills that empower the client to form healthier patterns in all their relationships (these will be discussed in Part Two).

RET is effective whether we have extensive knowledge of

the background, family histories or in the client's interpretations of past events, since it is not our intention to diagnosis or label clients nor their behaviors.

As RET technicians, we are interested in identifying the presently trapped negative emotions which have evolved from these experiences. We look for objective, factual information about the unprocessed trauma.

What is Rapid Eye Technology?

Rapid Eye Technology (RET) is a completely safe, drug-free process that seems to duplicate a natural process you do every night during REM (rapid eye movement) sleep.

RET is a revolutionary breakthrough in the treatment of emotional stress of all kinds and has effected lasting change in many peoples' lives.

Trauma induced memories in the unconsciousness, stored within the mind-body system, including the genetic material, cause distorted perception and irrational behavior in the present time. These memories include our basic beliefs and survival instincts. They effect our emotions and our self esteem.

These memories can limit our choices at an unconscious level. The ability to act rationally becomes diminished. Potential for self-development becomes restricted. Stress becomes detrimental.

These memories can be released (and re-framed) through Rapid Eye Technology!

There are many models of therapy which will bring painful experiences to the surface awareness, to assist a person in addressing the experience. RET works well in conjunction with all methods of healing because it **simply discharges the pain and emotions of these experiences!**

The RET model has as a premise, that you must process

22

trauma on many levels: mental trauma at the mental level, emotional trauma at the emotional level, and physical trauma at the physical level. Likewise, to *simply read* a book about dysfunctional behaviors would be an inadequate way to overcome the emotional or physical effects of the dysfunction.

RET technicians are trained in the mechanics of assisting clients in processing and releasing traumatic memories. **We are not professional counselors!** Although we are sometimes referred to as "healers", we are not healing anyone of anything. We are simply assisting clients in their own healing journey, utilizing the technique we have developed. Each person heals him or herself. RET is a process of releasing emotional and physical stress through movement of the eyes. This movement effects physiological functions as the cells in the body are allowed to release trapped life-force energy that has been manifesting as physical and emotional stress.

We have students in our trainings from many walks of life, with various levels of skill. Many of our technicians were professional psychotherapists prior to receiving their RET training and are using RET in conjunction with other methods of healing with their clients. We also have other professionals in related fields, as well as students, who have witnessed the powerful change in their lives after doing their own healing through RET processing and are dedicated to learning skills which will assist others in releasing pain.

Traumatic Memories

At the core of Rapid Eye Technology is the understanding of *traumatic memories*. This memory is defined as a survival decision about life that is trapped in unconscious memory by trauma activated by a trigger mechanism. The trauma may be physical, emotional, or both. The "trigger" is any sensory input that ties the current experience to the traumatic memory, thereby bringing the past trauma into the present experience.

When trauma occurs, the subconscious mind makes survival decisions on the animal level, and imprints those decisions as high-priority messages within the animal or primal brain. It is an automatic response mechanism. These are some of our most primal thoughts. Included with the primal brain is the limbic system, which is known to control emotions. Feelings of anger, rage, depression, fear, apathy, terror and sorrow all reside within this primal area.

It is our belief that on the physical level, the primal brain is the seat of most—if not all—our traumatic memories. The ingredients necessary for these memories are trauma (physical or emotional) and receptivity. The degree of receptiveness of the mind has to do with the energy level of the person. When a person's energy level drops to a sufficiently low level, he becomes receptive to traumatic memory, and looks at life totally differently than he would at a higher level of energy. He is "hooked" into that pathway of memory and he continues to act out.

Fetuses, infants, and small children are in a developmental mode and are thus automatically receptive to new programming via traumatic memory.

A traumatic memory is a trauma induced neural connection that produces a distortion or aberration wich results in a breakdown of communication in the mindbody connection. These physical distortions or aberrations are based upon significant emotional elements.

The emotional element is based upon a mental level traumatic memory and survival decision made at the time of trauma. To the extent that this mental decision, emotional element, and physical distortion can be addressed consciously the person experiencing it can be healed. Because these trauma induced memories contain a triggering element within them (to speed survival instinct along) we find ourselves triggered into a reliving of these traumas whenever we undergo a similar experience in present time. Many of us live most of our lives in this state, living the past in the present. It becomes an instinctive "knee jerk" reaction.

RET offers us an opportunity to discover these distortions and traumatic memories, bring them into conscious awareness, and discharge the emotional element associated with them. Because the body does not view these traumatic elements as distortions, it fails to reprogram or change them. So far as the body is concerned, "all is well", even when we are in great pain. The body is still doing the best it can under the circumstances. So far as it knows, there is nothing wrong with the system: all is functioning as it should. As the poem *"Turning the Tide"* says: "you adjust to the condition...it is normal for you..."

If we are to change any part of the mindbody system, we must first identify it on a physical level (so the body understands) what's wrong. The body is unaware of "effective" or "ineffective", so we must listen to what it is saying and teach it to heal.

Trauma can come in a number of ways. For one person, the trauma can be simply the look given by a parent; for another, the sting of a belt across the buttocks; and, for a fetus, it may pick up the trauma its mother is going through. Much trauma is inflicted as a part of child rearing by loving parents who lack the understanding of how the experience may be affecting their child (see *"Babies Remember Their Birth"*, by Chamberland).

Traumatic memories are hidden from conscious awareness, being instilled in the animal, or unconscious, part of us. Only the higher brain functions include conscious memory. This is meant to be a protection device so that we do not have to wallow in trauma all our lives. Normally we forget or "stuff" traumatic incidents in order to spare us from constant pain. A traumatic incident may be triggered often enough to keep our subconscious pain at a conscious level. Nevertheless, the cause of the pain is yet below conscious awareness, being hidden from higher thought in the primal brain.

The brain knows where each of these traumatic memories resides. Until just recently, with the development of RET, we did not know the technology to call them forth into consciousness, discharge the trapped energy and reprogram them through a conscious positive reframe.

Traumatic memories are at the root of irrational, negative behavior. They are the cause of illness, accidents, injuries, psychosis, neurosis, multiple personalities, obesity, colds, allergies, depression, addictions, abuse and much more.

The distortion actually creates toxins in the body at the physical and emotional levels. Once the conscious mind realizes the illusion of the traumatic memory, it can process it appropriately and release the toxin.

Honoring the Client

RET is about honoring and caring for the client. We genuinely love and care for our clients. We honor them in their journey. We provide for them, to the best of our ability, a safe and nurturing environment for healing. We offer the client the best technology we can. It is our intention to honor, love, care for, offer empathy, encourage, strengthen, and emotionally support our clients.

RET is best suited for the emotional level of our being. To our knowledge it is the fastest and most complete means of discharge of negative emotional material available today. The emotional toxins discharged by RET come from the deepest parts of our psyches and are associated with all the other traumatic memories we have stored in our bodymind over our lifetime (and perhaps even over the lifetimes of our ancestors through the wonder of DNA). This ancestral genetic chain of significant emotional events is directly effected by the RET procedure. The present issue is addressed as well as all the underlying issues. When one works in an RET session with a present time complaint, all the underlying traumatic material is also addressed.

For example, the neural pathways are similar to a computer disk. When a computer disk is formatted, it sets up a gridwork (similar to little post box addresses). In our brain, some emotions and experiences (trapped feelings) are stored in one "post box" or "location", while others (anger) are stored in another location. We may be processing "trapped in the birth canal" and the mind will automatically bring up other incidents of feeling trapped which may be stored in the same location, i.e., trapped in the birth canal, trapped in the crib, trapped in a wrecked car, trapped in a relationship, etc.

Clients go through this amazingly fast and visual people see pictures and get instant connections, while others may get an inner sense of knowing and deep feelings of understanding.

The result of RET on fears and phobias, emotionally significant relationship problems, family issues, and personal trauma, is nothing short of phenomenal.

Physical, Emotional and Mental Bodies

The wondrous machine we call our bodies has for many generations confounded man. Since caveman days, he has felt that he was the victim of the environmental factors around him, including his own body. In fact, in most cultures, the body is seen as the enemy, causing untold pain and suffering. We seem to feel that for some mystical reason, we can abuse, neglect, and offend our bodies and that the body will simply

27

sustain us no matter what we do to it. Today, we fill our bodies with pesticides, preservatives, acids, over-refined substances, and drugs to name a few offending substances. We either exercise too much or too little. We keep our bodies awake on unnatural schedules disrupting its natural cycles. We place it in high and low density climates (like outer space and deep sea diving). We jump out of airplanes and climb high mountains. What a marvelous machine that endures the abuse we dish out!

For centuries mankind has known about the impact emotions have on our physical bodies. When we feel stressed out we suffer things like ulcers and headaches. When we feel depressed emotionally, we often feel depressed physically, too. The connection is too strong and obvious to ignore. Masterful works on this subject have been published for many years, including those of Dr. Depak Chopra and Louise Hay. We highly recommend their material.

Let's consider some well known facts and theories about the body. The body is connected to every cell within it by a network of information and energy. The job of the nervous system, including the Peripheral Nervous System (PNS), the Autonomic Nervous System (ANS), the Sympathetic Nervous System (SNS), and the Para-sympathetic Nervous System (PNS), is to cause communication to occur throughout the body. This elaborate system of communication can be damaged, causing the naturally smooth flow of information and energy to become blocked and distorted. Most of the damage is done during traumatic experiences. If, for example, a normal message from the brain to the muscles of the index finger is damaged by the trauma of an injury to the wrist, the finger may begin to function less effectively, if at all. The same principle applies to the entire body system: damage to the nervous system results in some distortion in the functioning of a part.

To be precise, the idea of "distortion" connotes a malfunction of the system, when in reality, the system is always operating at peek performance for the given situation.

The Language of the Body

The language of the physical body is symbolism. That is, it "talks" to us in metaphor. Consider what your body might be telling you if you feel a pain in your chest: could you be experiencing heartache or sadness there? Opening yourself to the possibility that your body could be "speaking" to you in its own language opens the possibility that you could "talk" back to it, conduct a "conversation" and perhaps "get the message" and heal from it.

On the physical level of understanding RET assists in this "conversation" process. The body knows what it is saying and you know what you are saying. It's just the difference in the body's languages that gets in our way. Once you know the language, it is merely a matter of mutual understanding. We refer to this as "balance".

The nervous system of the body shares this language with every other part of the body system. Feelings in one part of the body are instantly shared with every other part through this system of communication. It is most effective until there exists a distortion or block. Interestingly enough, the body knows where and of what nature all these distortions and blocks are. Even the blocks and distortions speak the same language as the rest of the body. Since RET is a natural system utilizing the body's own innate system of communication, it seems to be most effective in releasing emotional trauma held in the body.

29

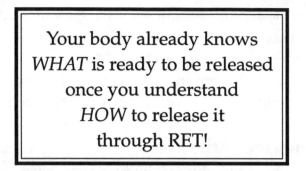

Your body already knows
WHAT is ready to be released
once you understand
HOW to release it
through RET!

The Use of the Eyes for Emotional Discharge

In the 1960s Evart and others discovered through their landmark studies on REM sleep that the body causes the eyes to move during certain important parts of the human sleep cycle. We postulated that the eye movement could be attributed to a neuronal expression of what is happening in the psyche of the client. That is, as the sleeper accesses and reorganizes unprocessed material in the visual, auditory and kinesthetic modes (Bandler & Grinder), his eyes move correspondingly.

J. Allan Hobson, Professor of Psychiatry at Harvard Medical School, and Director of the Laboratory of Neurophysiology, Massachusetts Mental Health Center, paraphrased Evarts saying, "The function of sleep may not be so much to rest the brain as to reorganize its information." On the subject of REM sleep, "While the brainmind is freed of the task of monitoring and remembering new information, in sleep it can review and reorganize its own already acquired data."

Observations of this phenomenon conclude that REM occurs every time a person achieves the alpha state, or Stage I of the normal sleep cycle (after about 90 minutes of sleep). In this alpha state the body is completely relaxed and the eyes are shut. Alpha is characterized by a relaxed feeling or meditation and dream state. This is the state most used in RET. Alpha waves are associated with a calm, lucid mental state. Alpha brain waves oscillate between 9 and 13 cycles per second.

Other states of consciousness used in RET that have known brain wave activity are:

1. The Beta state or waking consciousness. In this state, the attention is directed towards the external environment. These waves oscillate between 14 and 30 cycles per second.

2. The Theta state is found in states of deep relaxation. Theta activity is also associated with bursts of creative insight, twilight sleep, vivid mental imagery and deep meditation. Theta waves oscillate between 4 and 8 cycles per second.

3. The Delta state in which dreamless sleep occurs is characterized by deep profound relaxation. Delta waves oscillate between 1 and 3 cycles per second.

A client may experience all these states in a single session of RET which lasts 1 hour and 45 minutes.

For example, suppose when you are 5 years old and are about to run out into the street. It is raining and you see a large dog running toward you. Your mother yells at you to "stop" and your father runs up and spanks you to instill in your little child's mind to not run into the street. Your subconscious only records the experience as the following components; a) you are going to run into the street; b) it is raining, c) you see a large dog, d) your mother is yelling; and e) your father spanked you. Perhaps at later times you may experience any one of these elements and it will trigger this memory. The resulting feeling is fear and anger associated with the street. Each time this feeling is triggered, you will build a stronger neural pathway. Since the purpose of the subconscious is survival, from then on, any action involving a street will create a feeling of uneasiness which you may or may not associate with the original experience.

In RET, we move very quickly in order to get around the natural defenses of the conscious mind. Even though we may identify the feelings, the conscious mind can still say, "Oh! I can let that go. I now understand I can safely cross the street."

Eye Lid Blinking

Eye lid blinking cleanses and moistens the eye. It also stimulates the optic nerve with abrupt changes of light intensity. These physiological processes seem somewhat obvious. The psychological processes, however, are much less apparent. We know, for instance, that when an object approaches the face at high velocity and is suddenly checked short of impact, the eye lids will blink as part of a response called "flinching". In this case the blinking is a physiological response to a perceived danger to the organism. However, it is the psychological perception of peril that actually creates the reaction. This, therefore, is quite clearly a psychological response mechanism. Consequently we may postulate that blinking plays a psychological as well as a physiological role in our human experience.

Several theories have been posited to attempt to account for the psychological aspects of eye lid blinking. One hypothesis is suggested by the experience of Loewi who claimed he would solve intellectual problems in dreams. Perhaps when the eye lid is closed information is processed inward. During the eye lid open cycle of blinking a discharge is allowed outward. When the two parts of the blinking process are put together in rapid succession, an outward discharge followed by an inward ordering takes place. This process is then repeated with the next blink.

Another theory that seems plausible asserts that during the alpha state when the eye lid is opened, the mind discharges outward that which it is focusing upon. During the closed lid phase of blinking, the mind views a mirror that intensifies the emotional focus. Thus, the process cycles through mirroring (intensifying) followed by discharging (eye lids open), mirroring (closed), discharging (opened), mirroring, discharging, closed, opened, etc.

Regardless of the theory, the psychological benefit of eye lid blinking is dramatic and demonstrable. In other words, it works extreemly well to discharge trauma. When blinking is coupled with right/left brain accessing, the effect is extraordinary.

Each nerve cell looks much like a hand with a thin nucleus and from one to hundreds, sometimes thousands, of fingerlike projections called dendrites. It is through these dendrites that the messages of the body are passed from place to place. Since every cell in the body is connected through this system of dendrites and neurons, what happens to one cell is instantly communicated to all the others.

In the process of communicating sensory information to the cortex from the senses and other cells, the neurons pass the information along from neuron to neuron through the dendrites. Nerve cells exist in a fluid environment such that dendrites "float", having the ability to move and change position relative to one another. Neurons can also grow new dendrites and eliminate unused ones. This ability to grow new dendrites, eliminate unused ones, and change the position of those dendrites relative to other neurons creates neural pathways that some claim represents learned response to stimuli.

EEG readings at various points on the body show us that when a neural reading is taken in one place a similar neural reading will be observed elsewhere in the body as well. The messages which travel along the neural pathways are transmitted to the rest of the body by this marvelous networking.

Traumatic memories occur when the dendrites of one neuron fail to communicate correctly with its neighbors. The synaptic connections produced in response to trauma are always distorted causing incorrect messages.

For example, a rose may be sensed by the olfactory. That message was passed along to the cortex for computation and instruction to the body. If, in that pathway to the cortex, a traumatic memory were present, the message reaching the brain may not be "rose" at all. What may reach the cortex is "danger" or "death" or "anger", none of which is in the original message. In other words, the original message has been changed or distorted by a traumatic memory.

A good example of this principle is the association I made as a young child about the sweet smell of flowers at funerals. This created a message that the sweet floral smell means death and I could not be around lots of flowers for years. In fact it went even further, to cause me to be unable to even raise flowering plants. Once I healed this traumatic memory through RET, I no longer have this association.

This same process could cause trouble elsewhere, too. For example, a person may be suffering from a pain in his shoulder. If the neural pathways in the brain-shoulder connection include a traumatic memory, the cortex may get the message that, "I feel burdened," when the message given at the shoulder may very well be, "Send nutrients." In fact, the traumatic memory may be so complete that the cortex doesn't know how to respond so it simply shuts off the affected area.

Our research with RET has shown us there is a remarkable process which occurs when eye blinking is incorporated in the healing process. There is a phenomonal connection between the rapid blinking of the eyes and this repairing of the neural pathways which have been distorted by traumatic memories.

The eyes are truly the windows to the soul! Our natural ability to discharge emotional material with our eyes is only recently becoming accepted by the medical community. When we feel emotional upset we begin to blink at a different rate, the eyes get gritty or dry, and may burn or sting. When we think, our eyes move, sometimes imperceptibly in directions related to the eye accessing cues described in NLP (see the section on NLP).

We merely use this natural eye movement and reaction to emotion to the advantage of healing the client. The client is the actual healer in the process with the RET technician functioning more like a coach or assistant. We have learned quite a lot about what happens to the eyes during emotional episodes so we can assist the client in the discharge and reframing process. There are several natural therapeutic techniques we employ to assist the eyes in their innate healing functions. There are, in addition, several types of blinks we employ. Blinking is more than merely closing and opening the eyes. How hard you blink, how often you blink, and when you blink is significant to the RET technician. How your eyes feel during and after you blink is also significant.

We have discovered an effective pattern to perform before the face at certain times in the process. It is the eye-catching device that suggests to the brain where to "look" for significant emotional elements. It is this direction given the eyes through the blinking that makes this technique so powerful. The eyes are blinking out emotional trauma, reviewing significant emotional files in memory, genetic material, and connections to other people and lives. Together with the auditory input from the RET technician, this physical process of wand movement, blinking, and eye movement makes RET very quick and efficient. Emotions come to the surface and release almost immediately through the eyes.

There are times when an RET technician is unavailable or the next scheduled session is too far away and you are experiencing a stressful situation. We call this an emergency RET situation. There are self-help techniques that can be employed at a time like this. In our life skills classes, we emphasize the ability each of us has to deal with our own life experiences. Our bodies and minds are created to function in such a manner as to self purge, self heal. Knowing how to work with your own natural processes gives you the power to effect self healing. Clients become self-empowered...able to take care of the trauma of life.

We suggest that when you are feeling significant emotional stress that you seek out a trained RET technician and get help for yourself. When you are unable to do so and are feeling the stress, remove yourself from the stressful environment as soon as you can. When you are alone or in a stress free place, find two points on the wall in front of you and move your eyes to the perifery of your visual field.

These points will be on opposite sides of your center line: one far to the right and one far to the left. With your head held still move your eyes back and forth between the two points as fast as you can comfortably. Keep moving your eyes until the stress feels like it is lessening. When you feel a little better, breath deeply, hold the breath while you say the emotion aloud, then release the breath all at once out your mouth; do the breathing three times. See if you then feel much better. For further processing, make an appointment to see a RET technician soon.

This procedure of discharging emotional material with

a movement of the eyes is in keeping with the body's natural dishcharge process. Another method of bringing up and discharging emotional material is much slower, yet nearly as effective. This procedure has to do with the principle of abundance: what you feed will grow. If you will repeat out loud a hurtful phrase several times, you will tend to feel it more intensely. This intensity will tend to increase as the hurtful phrase is repeated. It will serve to bring the emotion to the surface where it can be discharged with the back and forth movement.

Case Study

Randy was five when he came home one day crying and scared. He told his father, a RET technician, that he had been attacked by a large black dog. Randy's dad, Ben, asked Randy to repeat his story again adding detail by asking leading questions (How did that feel? What happened next?). The boy was still crying, though, after repeating the story the second time, he was beginning to cry less. Ben encouraged Randy to cry and let it out, validating his son's emotional condition. Ben convinced Randy to repeat his story a third time and Randy began to get a little beligerent, "Dad, aren't you listening to me!!" Ben was undaunted, "Tell me more about the size and color of the dog". Randy recounted his experience repeatedly. By the fifth retelling, he was feeling much better and began to laugh, desiring to return to play with his pals outside.

Case Study

Elizabeth is a 27 year old black woman who had just nearly completed her early morning paper route when she was attacked by an unseen assailant. The man attempted to rape her, yet she escaped when a jogger came to her aid. She was a psychological mess when she appeared at her day job. Fortunately, her immediate supervisor had recently taken the RET training and was able to assist her by encouraging her to repeat her story several times then make an appointment with another competent RET technician (he wanted to avoid an employer-employee compromise). She was able to continue her paper route the next morning.

Where Did Rapid Eye Technology Come From?

Rapid Eye Technology (RET) is the result of many years of experience, trial and error, education, work, inspiration, and the encouragement of many friends, family and collegues. The premise of RET is that healing is necessary and can be done relatively less painfull because of the speed that you go through it. Years ago we accepted the idea that personal growth can eventually be done in joy rather than pain. In joy one can shift the perception and let go of pain (which, I might add, is much easier to say than to do in the beginning!).

The awakening to Rapid Eye Technology came in the 1980's while we were developing a slower, auditory, method. We had too many clients that were unresponsive to the slow method. We reasoned that there must be another way. It was under these circumstances that the inspiration came to use the eyes as a means of discharging negative emotion.

Initially, we were skeptical that a simple movement of the eyes would produce an emotional response. It was too "easy." We were accustomed to slower, proven methods of emotional discharge: shouting, screaming, crying, physical pains.

We had noticed the effects of eye exercises on family members involved in optometric exercises. (*"Seeing Beyond 20/20"*, Kaplan.) They seemed to feel so much better emotionally after they participated in these exercises. We discovered that the exercises consisted of a movement of the eyes laterally, diagonally, and vertically following the swinging action of a ball suspended from the ceiling. It was intriguing to investigate the possibilities involved in releasing emotion with eye movement. Research started to reveal the effects at different speeds of movement in front of eyes, combining mind-body with a verbal input to release it.

Shortly thereafter, we were introduced to studies that confirmed use of eye movement to discharge and release emotionally traumatic memories. Thereafter we found several studies that confirmed the idea. We believed that the accessing cues of the eyes (Bandler and Grinder 1979) contributed to an important aspect of our model of research. We felt that the direction the eyes moved was as important as the movement itself. Therefore, we continued an eye movement technology model that included multiple directions. We employed this model of eye movement (movement in multiple directions: laterally, vertically, diagonally) until 1989 when we had a client who could not move his eyes in any direction.

Case Study

John was convicted of child molestation three times and had served many years in prison. He was terrified to be out in the public because he feared the urges to re-offend were so strong that he was sure he would be put in prison for life.

John felt so ashamed and guilty. He would look straight ahead so that he didn't have to look directly at anyone. He had been coming in for about eight months before we tried to use the eye movement technology with him.

It was a first for us. In over a year of practice in the new model of eye movement we had not had a client unable to move his eyes back and forth! I tried every trick I could think of to assist John in moving his eyes, to no avail. He simply could not move them! He would move his head so that he would not have to move his eyes!

In a flash of inspiration, I told John to blink. He blinked rapidly for a short time and found he felt better and soon began to be able to move his eyes back and forth. It was a major break through! For the rest of John's session he blinked and moved his eyes back and forth. John had five such sessions before he placed himself on a maintenance schedule of one session per month. He has since lost all urges to reoffend. He is now living what seems to be a normal, productive life. Urges that once dominated his mind became only fleeting thoughts.

We discovered during the time we worked with John that the process worked more effectively when done very rapidly. In fact, it seemed the faster we worked, the more effective it became. We also found that we could do in two hours what would normally take us weeks to accomplish before. Clients were accessing emotional material and making connections so quickly that some were skeptical that they had participated in an emotional process at all. One man commented, "I don't think I did anything, it worked so fast, and all I did was blink." He did notice, however, that he felt better about himself and his family. Closer examination revealed that the body was indeed reacting as one does when asleep, organizing material and discharging it. I became very excited as I realized we may be duplicating the natural process of REM sleep in an awake state.

Case Study

Sharon came in depressed about her thirteen year old son who was acting out violently at home. She was referred by a friend who had received the old, slow model we had used earlier. Therefore, she had no knowledge of the style of technology we had recently been developing. She went away from her first session disappointed that she "did not get to complain and go over her problems." She did come back--this time with her son. After her second and his first session they were able to communicate with each other without screaming and fighting. She says, "This has saved my family! All I had to do was blink while my therapist moved an eye catching device, fed me verbal cues and telling me to 'let it go'. Amazing!" I also received all kinds of connections.

Heal and Teach Love

All along, the basic underlying purpose of Rapid Eye Technology and the people behind its development has been to heal and to teach unconditional love. For too long, we feel, people have suffered under the weight of judgment and conditionality. Awakening them to their true, loving, nature, free of the distorted view presented them through traumas and fears is the focus of Rapid Eye Technology. It is our commitment to continue investigating methods of healing to support this vision of global health. We envision the whole planet, indeed, all of mankind wherever they may exist, healed and whole in the moment.

Together with teaching new, effective living skills, Rapid Eye Technology offers clients a less painful journey to Self discovery: the discovery of the Real Self, the Inner Master, that resides within us all. Indeed, we are already OK. We need do nothing but release the trapped trauma and move into the love that is already within us. When one learns that it is possible to learn and grow through joy as well as pain, he begins to create an abundance ol love. He becomes the healing salve of his own world. RET works to remove the old hooks that seem to cause us to repeat old patterns of pain.

RET Components

The RET process deals with providing a way for trapped, distorted emotional messages to be processed or released from the cellular level within the physical body. We all have messages which entered the body through the emotional DNA at conception. This allows the accessing and processing of information which has been guarded by the subconscious throughout much of our lives. In fact, many researchers believe that most of our concepts or world views come from conception, gestation and birth.

We strongly believe the mind and body were created to heal themselves. They were also created to recycle and process all experiences in such a way that we could gather information and develop wisdom. Science and nature have taught us that nothing is ever lost, it only changes form. It is my belief that the wisdom gained during an entire lifetime is not lost. We literally have the imprinted experiences of our parents, our grandparents—all of our ancestors—in every cell of our bodies. This truly is *cellular memory*.

When unprocessed emotional pain is stored or stuffed, it distorts the body's ability to recycle and remain well. There have been many studies that indicate that a particular pattern will continue to run in a family until the pattern is broken or resolved. Unfinished business from an ancestor can affect our lives and actually shows up in the DNA and the eyes (see *"What the Eyes Reveal"*, Denny Johnson). As we release unprocessed emotional toxins, we are healing the pain of untold generations and we give that gift of healing to our decendents.

Breathing and RET

For centuries man has realized the value of proper breathing techniques to enhance health and well-being. Since oxygen is a vital element in cell structuring, it can be concluded that more oxygen to the cells means healthier cells. However, it actually goes beyond that. Energy derived from the air we breathe is fundamental in the coding and decoding of DNA molecules within cell structure.

When cells are deprived of sufficient airborne energy, the DNA weakens, producing, in effect, an inhibitor responsible for shutting down the ability of the cell to replicate. It is similar to placing a condom on the reproductive process of the cell. The condition is not permanent, however, and can be reversed.

RET processes the emotional toxins at a cellular level in our body which is most effectively accessed while we are in an alpha state. In order to achieve an alpha state, we use proper breathing as a means to relax and still the body. The fast movement of the wand also assists in putting a client in an alpha state.

Breathing is a very energetic life force-increasing technique. It can be used anywhere in the therapy to increase energy and to aide in releasing pain and emotion. There are basically six types of breathing used with RET:

1. **The Cleansing Breath:** The cleansing breath is done by filling the whole body with air in one deep inhale through the nose into the stomach and then expelling it all out through

the mouth at once.

2. **The Releasing Breath:** The releasing breath is done by inhaling through the nose until the chest is full of air, then while saying the painful phrase which is being released, purging the air from the lungs.

3. **The Physical Pain Breath:** The physical pain breath is a short pant, like a dog pant, repeated as needed.

4. **Energy Breath:** Close one nostril and breathe through the other nostril with middle finger on forehead between the eyebrows. Hold it then breath out the other nostril. Reverse and repeat several times. Also visualize breathing energy from above your head as you inhale, then breathe out your mouth as you exhale.

5. **Balancing Breath:** Image yourself breathing energy up from earth into the heart as you inhale through the nose and down from the sun through the mouth as you exhale.

6. **Continuous Breathing:** Breathe deeply in and out through the nose. Make this one continuous motion with no pausing between inhale and exhale. This should be continued for several minutes until tingling occurs. This method of breathing is used with the neurological integration (see next section). This increase in oxygen will send nutrition to the cells and begin to loosen any emotional blocks.

The theory behind the breath work is that when we conduct RET processing we focus positive energy into those cells through the thought process and proper breathing. As each cell is energized with oxygen and the block is removed, it is then given permission to release, and the body responds.

Neurological Integration

Neurological Integration was coupled with RET, providing a powerful way to access deep emotions and reframe traumatic experiences. This process was coupled with the inner child work along with a method of continuous deep breathing.

The process of Neurological Integration is a relatively new technique to the scientific and psychological fields. The studies we found referred to the process as Neurological Bonding. They suggested accessing energy caused by negative experiences. We have integrated this process, using reinforcement of the perfect energy within each of us at birth (or a binding with unconditional love). We call it *Neurological Integration*.

First developed by Dr. Kenneth Fabian of Portales, New Mexico, the study of Neurological Bonding (which we refer to as Integration) consists of visio-neuro-psychological processes utilizing the psychological bond between the eyes, the brain, and the pineal gland. Neurological integration has been with man since the beginning of time. Little is known concerning the physiological processes involved, though use of this procedure has shown dramatic results in almost every client who has been through the process.

Basically, we believe that the connection between the pineal gland (a higher order brain function) and the basal brain (including the limbic system) is immature in most humans. These and other brain functions normally integrate in the first three months of life, and thus create the potential for mature connections.

Once a person is integrated, it generally takes between 10 to 12 two-hour sessions, depending on the intensity of the issues, to make these mature connections and go through the birth and inner child stages. The mind in every case takes the client through stages of birth trauma and processes up to their maturity.

Each of us has within us the ability to feel and express deep affect emotion. Deep affect emotions are those that are primary to our being. Emotions such as grief, deep sorrow, apathy, fear, etc., are all deep affect emotions. These and other emotions that originate deep within us often surface in the form of irrational behavior—something like a pressure cooker relief valve.

To process these deep affect emotions, our bodies have incorporated a system of relief and communication we call neurological integration. This process was designed to occur naturally, and sometimes this does not occur for one reason or another.

These and other brain functions normally integrate (make mature connections) in the first sixty to ninety days of life. The physiological theories behind Neurological Integration are difficult to substantiate, however, we know that something physiological is occurring because we can actually view the changes in the eyes of the client and observe the processing they immediately begin to do. Many clients also feel the energy exchange. Many people are birth integrated, and they, of course, are the people who handle stress and trauma amazingly well because they are processing on a deep level already.

When an infant is born into the world it is in a fast growth period. All brain circuits are as yet basically untested and unused. Within the first six months of life a neurological whirlwind within creates a mass of cortex and neuropathways. It is truly miraculous. It is also a time when a baby is learning at an accelerated pace. The baby learns how to make noise, move, see, taste, and feel. Inside this infant's skull tremendous growth is occurring.

Brain cells that now replicate themselves will, after this initial six month period, cease to do so. The limbic system at the top of the primal brain stem is developing from its pre-birth rudimentary debut. Learning is the order of the day at this stage of development.

In order for the new organism to properly communicate from primal self to higher emotional self, it will have to develop a means of intercourse between the two. This is not an automatic function like growing an arm or hair. This connection between the animal and human brain is a learned operation. The question arises then, from where does one learn to communicate between his higher and lower emotional brain activities? From whom did we learn to walk?

We learned just like we did with arithmetic or reading: from someone who already knew how. Within the first ninety days of life a baby may become neurologically integrated by his mother, father, grandparent. It seems to happen better if the baby is familiar with the sound of voices from the womb. (See *Babies Remember Their Birth*, by David Chamberland). Later in life, a non-integrated person may become integrated through the same process with a person who is already integrated.

Studies on the affects of integration upon adults have revealed that all persons suffering from psychosis are non-integrated. Most people suffering from severe neurosis are also non-integrated. So what is integration and how does it affect the body?

The brain is capable of learning to bond with deep affect emotion, the process of communicating between higher and lower brain emotionally, by seeing another person's method of integration or processing energy.

In other words, the non-integrated person looks into the eyes of the integrated person and an energy exchange takes place and the mind says, "Oh, that's how its done!" Communication between the two brains occurs and then proceeds to promote the physiological growth necessary for such communication to continue.

Without neurological integration a person may become

frozen in time emotionally. Usually the emotional freeze time occurs at some time early in life, most often within months of birth.

Without neurological integration a person is unable to mature his emotions. This explains why we have adults with compulsive and childish behavior. They have not learned how to process experience and glean the learning from them. Many adults have no idea how they feel, much less an understanding of why they feel what they feel.

Within the arena of Rapid Eye Technology, neurological integration allows clients to contact and discharge heavy emotion much easier and much faster.

During the first or second session with the client, the RET technician will perform the integration. When the pineal gland is "turned on" to process emotions, the client is able to quickly begin lifting the emotional toxins which have been trapped at the cellular level. This occurs through the eyes.

The swiftness with which a client is able to contact emotion and discharge it is greatly enhanced with integration. It is our belief that Inner Child work is virtually impossible to ever complete on a deep level without integration.

It has been our experience that clients who become neurologically integrated return immediately to birth and begin processing deep affect emotion.

The recently integrated individual may experience tremendous emotional and physical upheavals. Once a person is integrated it is important for them to receive RET, since the experience can create further discomfort as distortions of trapped, unprocessed emotion rise to the surface. RET will enable the client to process and release the energy at a faster rate.

RET speeds up the process and takes off the heavy charge of emotion the person receives going through conception, gestation and birth, and other trauma received from birth to the present. Integration is a great aide to RET, just as RET is a great aide to integration.

What happens that keeps it from happening naturally? Our increasingly fast-paced world creates less and less of a family-based society. Unprocessed emotions in one person creates an environment where distortions are predominant and they develop fragmented relationships, which foster more unprocessed emotions. Children are born into this atmosphere and integration fails to take place until you have entire generations of people who are unskilled and unable to process the experiences of life.

Inner Child Work

The most important relationship we will discover within us is the relationship we have with the many personalities inside us. We often call this inner child work because we deal with all the little children we have been through different growth stages in our lives. Within each of us is the child we were when we were a youth. Most of us go about our daily lives emotionally existing as a child of less than six. We are not aware of the stymied emotional growth because we seem to be "normal", or just like everyone else. That is so because most of our neighbors and friends, co-workers and family members are operating from the same level of emotional maturity.

Wouldn't it be wonderful to "grow up" emotionally? At the very least, wouldn't you like to find out what emotional maturity feels like? Most of us are being held captive by a two year old within. Specific RET techniques have been developed to deal expressly with the child within. Within each of us is the child that didn't quite grow up. We joke about it at times and even chide one another about it with, "Grow up!" and, "Act your age!"

With RET the little child within each of us can grow up without losing identity or value. As we get in touch with that inner child, we begin to truly discover who we are. You were born to be loved, and you are capable. Many of us didn't get what we needed the first time around. Discovering the child within can happen very fast and effectively with RET and the separation can be healed.

Case Study

Karen is a twenty-one year old woman who has a very demanding job in accounting. She was finding it increasingly difficult to concentrate on her work and had undergone psychiatric evaluation and found that her IQ was unusually high and her abilities to work were very good. She was perplexed that she was having so much difficulty in her chosen career. She had even thought of going into another field of work, yet she loved what she was doing and she was unsure that she could do any other work without difficulty, too. She was really feeling perplexed.

In her first session of RET she discovered that she had been trapped at the age of two by a traumatic memory. Her RET technician had begun RET treatments in a standard manner switching immediately to work on her inner child situation. In one session Karen was able to recover her lost inner child that had been controlling her so strongly in her adult life. She continued her inner child work with RET bringing her up to present time and age within six sessions. She has since found many other issues to work on and continues RET because she is excited to help her family.

Many clients find the work of RET so enjoyable that they continue with RET after immediate issues have been addressed and they work toward further personal growth.

The significance of the family system in the our lives

must be addressed. Many of the wounds we carry were inflicted within that structure. As we come to understand how we were affected, we can begin to heal the lost child within and remember our own perfect and whole nature. The role played by us in our family and the role played upon us by our family is all important to us.

Within the arena of family systems John Bradshaw and others have identified roles relegated to family members in a dysfunctional system. Further, most of us would acknowledge that all families are dysfunctional to some degree. (For more information on this subject we would recommend John Bradshaw's *Focus on the Family* series.)

Essentially, family members play important roles for each other so that we may grow and progress in this dimension of physical experience. When we are free to choose our role we grow more rapidly and with more appreciation than when we are assigned roles to fulfill. This is the significant difference a dysfunctional family system imposes upon its members: **roles are assigned rather than chosen.** This is due to the controlling nature of the system.

The dysfunctional family system is one that has been in the making for generations. Dysfunctional families tend to generate dysfunctional families. That is, addiction begets addiction, abuse begets abuse. What one generation unwittingly does to another is often carried on to the next generation and the next and the next, ad infinitum. Unless...

The cycle of dysfunction can be broken if someone in the family system learns to release the collective stored emotional trauma through an effective psychological process like RET. With RET we can effectively address the dysfunctional family system and release trapped emotional trauma from the control issues involved in the system. More importantly, through the second half of RET, the cognitive work, new skills can be developed which will break the patterns and allow family members to create more healthy relationships.

Additionally, besides the family system as a whole, there are significant personal issues to address. The order in which a person enters the family system and the place they take within that system as they mature is of importance to the process of emotional healing. Miller states that we "come into our families to serve and heal". While you might feel that the reverse is true, see if the following fits you and your family situation:

Birth order and significance:

First child: comes to serve the Father. This child reflects to the father what the father unconsciously needs and denies.

Second child: comes to serve the Mother. This child mirrors to the mother what she unconsciously needs and denies.

Third child: comes to serve the Father-Mother relationship. This child mirrors to the relationship what it needs and denies.

Fourth child: comes to serve the Family system. This child mirrors to the system what it needs and denies.

Fifth child comes to reflect the complete dysfunction. The subsequent children repeat the above order. Children born more than five years apart begin the order over. When children move out of the home, the next child replaces the one ahead of him/her, everyone moving up one place in the order. Children sometimes exchange patterns. Adopted children are the same as natural in their order. An "only" child will reflect back all five patterns. Look at your own family and see if this relationship may help you to learn from those who have come to serve you, and see if you are taking the feedback.

RET technicians are extensively trained on how to assist their clients in processing inner child issues by locating and releasing trapped trauma. It is not uncommon for clients to make significant connections to help them understand that they are actually "adult children" who have been "stuck" in one growth stage or another. Learning to love this part of themselves, the little lost child within, allows nurturing to occur in exactly the manner that brings healing. The inner child is living very much in the emotional body and cannot be healed from the mental level. This child will not be ignored! When it is wounded, it will keep acting out until it is noticed and loved. It is unlikely anyone truly heals who has overlooked or ignored this part of their work.

In order to effectively process childhood trauma, we have found it very helpful to understand how the brain processes information. For this reason, we include inner child work and Neural Linguistic Programming principles in our RET model.

Neural Linguistic Programming (NLP)

Brain researchers, like other scientists, have spent much of the 20th century engrossed in the linking areas of the brain, both in the cortex and in subcortical regions to the complex mix of perception, sensations and judgments we call emotion. These thoughts form neural pathways in the brain. Emotions are not just formed in the brain, but are directly linked to they lymphic system. This system is not limited to the brain; when we feel emotion, we feel it in our entire body.

In developing the RET model, we soon realized that releasing these toxic emotions from the lymphic system seemed to leave a vacuum. Knowing that the universe abhors a vacuum, we realized the importance of replacing the negative with the positive through all the levels of body, emotion, mind and spirit. NLP seemed to fill that void.

This programming was discovered by Richard Bandler and John Grinder. NLP works directly with this entire mind/body connection.

Basic to the NLP model is the concept that people process information in a number of ways. Basically, we input data via our five senses: sight, sound, touch, smell, and taste. Of these five inputs, most people tend to favor three: sight (visual), sound (auditory), and touch (kinesthetic).

As babies we input through all our senses fairly evenly. Babies put everything in their mouths in order to taste it. They are busy smelling, hearing, seeing and touching everything in their environment. Babies experience life totally and are constantly in the present moment.

As an individual grows older, however, they tend to develop a favorite mode of processing or inputting data. For some of us, sight is all important. We may feel like we would die without sight. Everything must be seen in order to be experienced. If sight is removed, however the mind will develop another way to process. These types of people are referred to as "Visual."

When we are accessing information that is to be visually remembered or recalled, we look up to the left. These are things we have seen before, such as the color of our mother's eyes. When we are accessing new information that is to be visually constructed, we look up to the right. These are things we are creating visually.

When we are accessing information that is to be auditorially recalled, we look directly to the left side. These are things we have heard before, such as the sound of our grandfather's voice. For an auditory person, hearing is all important. They love to talk and listen. Music has a special meaning for them. They prefer to hear things said rather than to see them drawn or pictured. These people will listen very intently to the sound of your words and notice how your sentences are constructed. We call these people "Auditory."

When we are accessing information that is to be auditorially constructed, we look directly to the right side. These are things we have never heard before and are thus imagining.

When we are having an internal dialogue with ourselves, we look down and to the left. These are things we are saying to ourselves, such as reciting a favorite poem to oneself or reprimanding ourselves for making a mistake. A person who is depressed spends much of their time with their head down and looking to the left.

People who prefer to experience their reality via the sense of touch are often referred to as feeling people. They prefer to get in touch with things. They often speak slower than do auditory or visual people. We refer to people who prefer to feel their experiences of life as "Kinesthetic." When they are accessing their feelings, they look down and to the right. They are accessing things they are feeling emotionally, tactually (sense of touch), or feelings of muscle movement.

There is no preferred orientation of representational systems. We each use all three representational systems all the time. However, we tend to favor one over the others. In fact, we normally use a combination of systems in our every day experiences.

We use NLP with RET very effectively. The study of NLP gave us the knowledge of eye movements, modes of accessing information, anchoring (trapping that positive feeling or image for future reference), reframing or redefining emotions and meanings.

Sometimes the eye accessing is quite rapid, sometimes it is not. Always, however, the eyes will contact the brain according to the system being employed. The previous examples seem to be for right handed people. It may work the opposite for left handed people.

It is said that the eye is the window to the soul. We use the eyes in this manner with our RET model. The eyes can also be used to identify which representational system is currently being utilized. Eye accessing cues tell a lot of the story going on in the client's mind, as well as the patterns in the eyes. Negative energy is primarily released through the eyes.

Energy appears in many forms. The universe is filled with energy. Everywhere one looks there is energy. Within our bodies are billions upon billions of cells comprised of billions of molecules which are in constant motion creating constant energy. Our bodies even create heat from the fuel we give them. Energy seems to have only two polarities. That is, energy is either positive or negative, plus or minus, yin or yang. Energy exists on all four planes of known human existence.

We create thought energy also. Thought energy is of a different sort since it cannot be perceived by normal sensory input. It is, nevertheless, real.

Each time we are denied or we deny ourselves the opportunity to discharge or express pain, we stuff our trauma and create the emotional distortion that will later come back to haunt us. When we get into crisis, it is beneficial if we can receive emergency processing, or a chance to tell our story over and over until the charge is gone. As we discussed earlier, each trapped energy must be released on its own level--physical, emotional or mental.

Of our five senses, the eyes are the most sensitive to energy. Any energy change in the body is reflected in the eyes. The optic nerve goes directly into the brain and connects directly with the basal brain and the lymphic system. The blinking process used with RET does effect the total mind/body connection.

After visiting a holistic health fair where I was able to see a demonstration of Kirilian film, which shows the body's energy field, we realized how important working with this energy field could be with the RET process.

This energy field is discussed in Barbara Brennon's Book, *"Hands of Light"*.

Reiki

At about the same time, I came across a system of working with the human energy field. The system is called Reiki.

Reiki was developed by a Japanese doctor named Mikao Usui. After hearing Dr. Usui's history and having an experience with Reiki, I took the training at its different levels up to and beyond mastership. We then began to integrate it with RET. The results have been astounding. We now teach Reiki as well as RET at our centers.

As the body releases and discharges energy, it is released into the energy field. Reiki assisted us to release and clear the negative energy trapped around the body.

Reiki is not required for every therapist to know, yet energy work of any kind is effective and beneficial and gives the technician additional tools to help the client.

Therapeutic Touch, Shiatsu, and massage are all other ways of working and releasing that have been used effectively with RET.

Light, Sound and Color

The use of light and sound technologies has been a wonderful adjunct to the RET model. We have found that the addition of blinking lights or solid colored lighting in conjunction with tones can be very effective. What the lights and sound do to the psyche seems to be similar, but does not take the place of

RET. We have only recently incorporated light, color, and sound with the blinking process of RET. It has been very effective and we expect to see further developments as research and experience continue with this exciting new frontier. The effect of the light/sound equipment on clients with addictive behaviors has been heartwarming to us. We always monitor clients while they are under the lights. We will sometimes administer the light/sound technology to two or three clients in different rooms. We will check on them periodically and generally finish each session with RET to assure any "lifted" energy is released. Many clients like this kind of arrangement because they benefit from the lights and sound as well as working with a trained technician.

The light/sound equipment often brings up deep emotional responses and can be used to bring up hidden emotions. These deep affect emotions can be very disconcerting to a person if he feels he has no one to be there to assist him through it. It is helpful to have a trained RET technician on hand to assist when this happens. This usually is needed only in the beginning after RET sessions. People can use the light and sound on their own.

Imagery

Imagery is drawing on the mind's ability to create, and is very useful in RET for not only reframing, but for moving through blocks and seeing with the inner eye.

An example of the power of imagery can be shown through the following example:

Imagine yourself on a tropical beach. The surf is rolling in to shore, the smell of flowers floats delicately on the air. The warm sun on your skin is soothed by the cool, gentle breeze. Notice the feelings in your body from imagining this scene.

Now imagine this:

It is dark, cold night. You are standing alone by the tracks in a rail yard. You hear off in the distance the whistle of an approaching train, you see the lights begin to get brighter and brighter. Suddenly the train is in front of you, roaring by at top speed.

Notice how that made you feel. How did that differ from the first experience?

Albert Einstein expressed emphasis on simplicity when he said, "The simpler our picture of the external world and the more facts it embraces, the stronger it reflects in our mind the harmony of the universe." Mental vibrations crystallize as "things". The theory of bioplasmic energy suggests that the entire universe known to the mind is composed of vibrations.

Finer vibratory rates are perceived by the mind as thought. When the vibrations in the mind get coarse and alter their pattern, the mind creates the impression of things out there in space. The mind creates vibrational patterns into images.

The practical aspect of this lies in the idea that by altering the rate of vibration or thought, the mind can alter the state of the matter constituting its environment.

This ability of the mind to affect matter in space occupied by the body has enormous implications for healing. Imagery increases energy—negative or positive—and is most powerful if done in a relaxed alpha state.

With RET, clients are urged to see themselves as whole and healed in the moment. Start by knowing you are OK, seeing yourself already healed. This brings the trauma quickly up into the light to discharge or heal and trains the brain to function that way. The mind only knows what we think, and will act accordingly, thereby facilitating the process of healing.

Part Two

RET - Reframing Traumatic Memories

Cognitive Work

Cognitive work is the other half of the RET treatment. This part of the treatment cannot be overlooked! Educating the client to new living skills or tools is vital in the self-discovery work. We avoid labeling people or behaviors and we encourage clients to see themselves already healed and whole. This ability to see themselves as complete and whole is sometimes called faith, or acting "as if" (start by knowing you are already there). We have found it to be powerful!

We teach an ongoing class which helps clients not only identify non-productive beliefs, but they also become aware of the power they have within themselves to change the circumstances of their lives.

These new living skills or principles are taught in a course called "The Seven Principles", sometimes referred to simply as "Living Skills." It is about natural laws, or principles, which govern human development. This course of study covers the Principles of Thought, Perception, Cause and Effect, Choice and Accountability, Gratitude and Abundance, Health and Healing, and the Principle of Rhythm and Harmony.

To assist in achieving a complete understanding of the principles, they are taught on all levels: physical, emotional, mental and spiritual.

These classes help the client learn new living skills so they don't simply re-create experiences which take them back into the old habit patterns. Slipping back into old patterns is less likely if you have built new paths for your thoughts to follow.

The RET model is a powerful method of learning. Once the client begins to release trapped neural distortions through RET, it is vitally important to replace that non-productive energy with an enlightened set of new living skills. Many people are aware their life may not be working for them, but they have no idea how to go about changing their living patterns. It is difficult to change something you don't understand.

For instance, if you were to imagine yourself entering a huge shopping mall that you've never been in before, what is the first thing you do? You'll go to the directory and determine where you want to go. Once you locate the store you want to go to, you must determine where you are in relation to the location of the store.

Similarly, in any task you undertake to do you must first determine where you are before you can be effective in your efforts to achieve that goal. Mastering these laws or principles can forever change the course of your life experience.

Most of us are seeking a better understanding of ourselves and our world. Only by realizing it is time to grow do we open our minds to new ideas. These ideas are, in fact, new only to us. They have been around for centuries. Yet these concepts, when put into effect, can literally change our lives.

Many of us learn new skills to improve our jobs. Could we put the same effort into learning new skills that will improve our lives? It's been said most people spend more time planning their vacation than they do planning their life!

Consider the possibility of learning new life skills.

Basic to Rapid Eye Technology are seven principles (or laws) that govern growth. The Self Discovery Processing is a two-part therapy, with the cleansing of old programming through RET as only half the process. The other half of the therapy is learning and implementing new life skills. It is an opportunity to reframe and restructure old, negative, unsuccessful habits and beliefs into more positive, successful ones.

The principles are studied and understood on many different levels. In general, it isn't too difficult to understand how things work on a physical level. The emotional level becomes more difficult to understand, unless we work on old programming. The mental level is often the most difficult because it means giving up old beliefs and stretching comfort zones. Even when old programs have not worked in life, people still hang on to them. There seems to be comfort in the familiar path, even if it leads to destruction or a dead end.

No lasting success in life is separated from enlightened living. A thorough understanding of these principles will allow you to move into alignment with the natural consequences of correct principles. I firmly believe these principles can become part of anyone's life. To learn them on the physical, emotional, mental, and spiritual levels, it is necessary to enter a higher state of understanding.

> Einstein observed:
> "The significant problems
> in our lives cannot be solved
> at the same level of understanding
> we were at when we created them."

As we develop our understanding sufficiently to solve a specific problem, it naturally raises us to the next skill level. We are then capable of creating a problem at this new level. This stimulates us to continue to develop our understanding to solve the problem, and we continue to grow to an even higher skill level. This upward spiral of learning is what propels us on toward self discovery in its greatest sense.

It is impossible to impart knowledge unless you personally possess it. Intellectual knowledge is the starting point. The deeper knowledge comes from the ability to pattern ones own life according to the principles of greater learning. Your success will be directly proportionate with your ability to not only *understand*, but also to *implement* higher living skills into your daily life.

Learning and the acquisition of knowledge are excellent motivators to change our lives. The reality is: the only thing we really can change is our mind. Fortunately, our mind is our most powerful tool! It is important to discover what works for you.

As you become versed in the principles of growth, you will see greater value in RET. Learning, teaching and living the principles will cause you to become more efficient in your healing and in your life in general, particularly once the trapped energy is restored.

The following pages concerning the seven principles of growth are merely a start towards understanding. The principles, rather than a religious or moral code, are shared from the experience gained by many individuals over many lifetimes. The principles work independent of belief, so I suggest you experiment with them. Give them a chance. You have nothing to lose and everything to gain!

What Are "The Principles"?

1. The Principle of Thought: We create our reality with our thoughts. Thought is completely free and we can think anything we want to think at any time. Thought is boundless by time and space. It is the primary mover of all creation. Energy follow thought in order to create!

2. The Principle of Perception: Since our thoughts create our reality, our perception is how we sense that reality. Our perception is always effected by how we understand and filter our past, and then bring that into our present environment. Perception allows things to be neither right nor wrong. It just "is", based on our experience and programming of life. One person's perception is as appropriate for him or her as mine is for me. Both people can be right at the same time, based on their experience.

3. The Principle of Choice and Accountability: We can choose anything we wish. We are not free to choose the consequences of our choices, those have already been set by the universe. When we become disenchanted with one choice, we can simply choose again (a perception shift). Choosing again will not short circuit the playing out of the consequences of a previous choice. We are accountable for the choices we make. Choice and accountability, as a unit, equates to the development of personal empowerment

4. The Principle of Cause and Effect: What we think about will be created (go out from us) and return again to us multiplied. In other words, we are the creator and the created, the first and the last, the cause and the effect. All creations must return to their creator.

5. The Principle of Abundance: Whatever you feed will grow. Interrelated with cause and effect and choice and accountability, abundance shows us that gratitude is the only appropriate response to life and the basis for more abundance. The universe is set up to provide us with experience in abundance in whatever form we choose.

6. The Principle of Health and Healing: We are responsible for our own physical, emotional, mental, and spiritual health. We sustain ourselves in each of these levels of being with proper nutrition, proper exercise, and proper cleansing on each level.

7. The Principle of Harmony and Rhythm: All universal laws or principles work together in complete harmony. All life exists in a "one-song" of rhythm presenting a musical vibration that creates perfert balance such as one might find in a symphony orchestra. It is our essential nature to flow with the universe, to be "at one ment". It is only the false ego states, developed from birth as we come into a laboratory of learning that is based on opposition, that creates the resistance to the natural flow of the energy of life. It is only then that we may even think in terms of being "out of balance".

You may or may not have heard these principles before. You have never before been the person you are right now. You have never before been in the exact condition you are now: same age, same physical condition, same thought processes, same understanding of life. So, open up the windows of your own possibilities as we explore the unlimited realm of possibility with you.

The Principle of Thought

Think for a moment. Everything starts with a thought. Your home was first a thought in someone's mind. Your car started out in the mind of a designer or engineer. Everything that exists now was first a thought.

Since everything starts with thought, it follows that thinking creates. We are always thinking. There is never a second when we are otherwise engaged. Even in sleep or unconsciousness we are thinking. Muscles require sleep. Thought processes require no rest.

> "All thought is creative
> by its nature because
> energy follows thought,
> and matter follows energy. "

Some thoughts create corporeally, others die in the realm of thought. Some thoughts are meant to be manifest is our world, others are meant to remain thoughts only. Our thoughts reside in a realm that is free of the limitations of this world. That is, you are free to think anything. You can imagine anything. Since you can imagine or think anything you wish, you also can choose what you will think.

Since thought is always creative, we might consider the possibility that we can control what we create with our thoughts. We control our reality by controlling our thoughts.

Our world is exactly as we have created it. Dr. Deepak Chropra refers to the space between each thought as *"the silent realm of infinite possibilities"*.

All Thought is Creative

The principle of thought is...*all thought is creative*. We are creating our world at this very instant. It is precisely as we think it is. And the moment we take responsibility for our world will be the moment we take control of our world!

Thought is the principle that puts all other principles into motion. Nothing happens without thought. Sometimes we may think our thoughts are scattered, and we may be correct. Recognize that those scattered thoughts are always creating something.

All our worries, woes, troubles, enemies, poverty, and grief have all been created by us. Though we may point the finger of blame at someone else, we are doing the thinking in our world. Perhaps it's time we took responsibility for our thoughts and change our thinking! And so we can!

Start by realizing that our thoughts are free. We may think any thought we want to think at any point in time. So we could choose to imagine our world perfect, just the way we want it to be: safe, exciting, challenging, successful, warm, comfortable, peaceful, full of friends and loved ones. We could, if we wish, think of an enemy as a friend in our thoughts (only *we* can prevent ourselves from doing this). We can see marriage as perfect in our thoughts. We can imagine our boss giving us a raise, driving a new car, house, boat—we can imagine anything without limits. Choose to imagine life as we would like it to be. Then practice focusing our thoughts on that image. Act "as if."

To focus thoughts, remember all thoughts are energy. Energy vibrates at various levels of intensity and frequency.

Spiritual thought energy vibrates at a much higher frequency than does temporal, earthly, three-dimensional energy. In order for us to slow spiritual thought frequency down to manifest into our three-dimensional world, we must "hold it" until it is manifested.

> ## "Focusing on a thought slows its vibration. "

As we put energy (focus) into the thought, it becomes manifested in our three-dimensional world of substance.

Most of the time, however, we send out our thought vibrations in many directions at once, negating the effect of focusing. Therefore, our thoughts never materialize in this dimension and we feel frustrated. You're probably familiar with the feeling of working hard at something just to see it fall apart. Maybe it was a relationship or a project at work. It seems, at times, no matter what the work is or how hard we work, our expected outcome will fail to manifest in the way we want.

Traumatic memories are another thing that can stand in the way of focusing thought. When positive thoughts are negated with neural distortions, the result is frustration. It is possible, however, to clear out the traumatic memories in the realm of thought through high spiritual experience.

The RET process itself works in the realm of thought. We work with thoughts, rather than corporeal reality. RET is another way to clear these neural distortions.

A closed mind or negative feelings can also block thought. Truth is positive. It is forgiveness and love. It is knowing we are loved and worthwhile. We can free ourselves of the bounds of guilt and fear. See our great worth and let go of guilt. Learn to control our thoughts. When we identify with the power of our own thoughts, there is nothing we are unable to do, no obstacles we will be unable to overcome. Faith is this power! It can literally move mountains--in thinking and in our lives. If we fail to change our thinking, the mountains return.

Getting Control of Our Most Powerful Tool

Our mind is the world's most powerful instrument! By using our mind in the way we choose to think, we literally create our own world. If we change our mind, our behavior will change and so will our reality, our world.

Because the mind is the source of all of our experiences, we can always trace our life lessons back to a pattern of thinking. When we discover the pattern of thought that needs to be changed, the physical symptoms or manifestations will disappear, for their function as the communicator of a lesson is no longer needed.

Miracles are fruits of faith, or the process of acting "as if." How do we act as if? We begin by modeling, or imitating, the way we would behave if we had already achieved the result we are after. If our desired result was to be a great chef, we would study cooking and use the same recipes that the great chefs use. We wouldn't become a great chef by stirring together the same old box of macaroni and cheese every night.

As we begin to practice acting as if, it becomes more readily apparent that every thought we have makes up some segment of the world we see. It is with *thought* that we must work.

Every thought we entertain contributes to truth or to illusion. Either it extends truth--or it multiplies the illusion!

71

What is an illusion? Can we see our physical life as an illusion? If we did, would it make a difference in our thinking? No one can be a slave to two masters. With our thoughts wegive energy to the way our life will be. We must choose in which direction we want to sendyour thought energy.

Correction happens only at the level where change is possible. We can't protect our peace by protecting our thoughts. Recognize it is unnecessary to feel worried, afraid, or feel sorry for or be critical of ourselves or others. Realize doubting is the primary cause of many of our troubles.

Love is the way to see our perfection. We control our thoughts by controlling the focus of our attention.

The Flow of Thought

Creativity flows in this way: spiritual creation, mental creation, emotional energizing, physical manifestation. The reason so many of our thoughts fail to come into physical manifestation in our lives is that we judge them and discard them in our thoughts. The spiritual world is always creative, and the physical world is always obedient. It is only the thoughts, fortified with emotions, that make the cycle of creation complete or incomplete.

Our thoughts will naturally flow where our attention is focused. A famous English satirist was once asked if he would teach the art of caricature. He refused to do so.

"It is not a faculty to be envied," he explained. "Take my advice and never draw a caricature. You'll get into that habit and from then on nothing will look good to you. People have a face divine and that's what we should see."

Some people are caricaturists at heart without being artists. They habitually look for flaws in appearance as well as personality. They find a certain amount of pleasure in poking fun at person's nose, mouth, or mannerisms. Thus, they lose

72

the facility of seeing the good things, of seeing people as they are with the charm and beauty they really possess.

Belief begins with belief in ourselves. When we look in the mirror, we're looking at our best friend or our worst enemy. Our world revolves around us. It starts and ends in the heart. What we are and hope to become begins with belief in ourselves. We believed we could walk when we took our first step. We believed we could talk when we said our first word. We believed we could earn when we took our first job. We believed we could succeed and we probably did because we believed, or we failed because we believed we would fail.

> Henry Ford once stated,
> "Whether your think you can
> or whether you think you can't,
> you are right." And so it is.

Our whole life is based on belief-faith of one kind or another. We add to the growth and progress of our community when we believe in progress. We support law and order with our belief in fairness and justice. We help all people everywhere with our belief in them.

About Guilt

Guilt is the word we use to describe feelings of culpability, especially for imagined offenses or from a sense of inadequacy. Guilt is self-reproach. Synonymous with guilt are: sinfulness, shame, contempt, disgrace, dishonor, scandal.

The destructive nature of guilt is impossible to be

overstated. The mind of the "guilty party" immediately drops in consciousness when the perceived offense is recognized, severely limiting the ability of the conscious mind to function properly to overcome the shortcoming.

The next stage of guilt after recognition is blame. We realize that a scapegoat must be found to atone for the sin. That scapegoat is always ourself. We manifest the placing of blame on ourselves by dramatizing anger, illness, and pain. As we lower our consciousness to anger, we shut down the conscious mind to the point of becoming ineffectual. We need our mind clear to deal properly with shortcomings.

It is given to us as humans to be agents unto ourselves. It is important that we make mistakes and learn from them. If we chain ourselves down to the heavy weight of guilt, we place ourselves in a position of helplessness. Since we perceive that we are worthless when we are guilty, we look outward for anyone else to take the blame for us. We usually succeed in finding someone who is more than willing to take the blame. Though we think we have shifted responsibility for actions to someone else, it merely appears that way. What we have done is to give away our power to make a correction.

Many of us have been taught about guilt since we were little children. Our parents taught us to take upon us their sense of guilt. Our Sunday School teachers have taught us to take upon us guilt for our sins and sometimes, the sins of others, too. What are we to do?

First, recognize that guilt is an emotional response to feelings of inadequacy in ourselves. Armed with that information, we can dig out that feeling, correct it, and get on with life. Guilt may be perceived as a "bad" thing. It also may be viewed as a gift to us to help us recognize when we are out of alignment with our true self.

If we perceive guilt as a destructive element in our life,

correct our perception, release our feelings of inadequacy, and get on with living a life of fulfillment and peace.

Relationships

We can redefine ourselves and others with our thoughts. It is in our thoughts that we experience everything. All our feelings come from our thought, but the feelings or emotions that we generate are the connections to other thought or people. Most of us never think about the great power we have in our ability to think. All our relationships are connected by invisible thought. What we think about expands, and your thoughts originate within you. We always have the option to process any behavior—either ours or someone elses—another way.

Our relationships reflect how we relate to ourselves. What you experience inside of you gets there by thoughts. If we can look beyond the lesson that we or others are in and see the perfect spiritual being within, then we can love and lose the need to be controlling.

If we desire to change our thoughts and our life, then we begin by knowing we have already arrived, and the miracle will happen in our life.

Because so many people base their self worth on the opinions of others, we can help them change their lives when we see and treat them as perfect and complete divine beings already.

The Principle of Perception

The story is told of a philosopher who stood at the gate of an ancient city greeting travelers as they entered. One of them questioned him: "What kind of people live in your city?"

The philosopher met the question with a counter question: "What kind of people lived in the city from whence you came?"

"Oh, they were very bad people," answered the traveler, "cruel, deceitful, and devil-worshipping."

"That's the kind of people who live in this city," declared the philosopher.

Another traveler came by and asked the same question, to which the philosopher replied: "What kind of people lived in the city from whence you came?"

"Oh, they were very good people," answered the second traveler, "kind, and truthful, and God-loving."

The philosopher replied, "That's the kind of people who live in this city."

Perception is, in a nutshell, our beliefs based on our experience. The way we perceive our present-day world is based on how our world has been in the past, and the meanings we put on those experiences are based on that perception.

There is no "right" or "wrong" in perception. Perception simply "is"! It is made up of either *illusion* or *reality*. Illusion is defined as anything that is temporary in nature, that was thought up by man, and had a perception placed on it. When two or more people agree on this illusion, it then becomes their reality.

Perception can make whatever picture the mind desires. This is especially important to remember in the way we perceive others.

Whenever we judge anyone negatively, we are really judging those aspects in ourselves. It is impossible to see something in someone else unless we perceive it in ourselves on some level or experience.

Instruction in perception will help us realize there is always another way to look at any situation. With improved perception we can avoid judging others.

There were five blind men who were asked to give their best judgment of an elephant, based upon the perception of their experience. One, after feeling the elephant's tail, declared that certainly an elephant was like a rope. The second protested, having touched the trunk and concluding the elephant was undoubtedly like a snake. The third man bumped up against the elephant's tusk and stated conclusively that this animal was like a spear.

The elephant flapped his ears and the fourth was assured that the elephant was like a fan. The fifth man wrapped his arms around the elephant's leg and tried to lift it. He was fully convinced that this was a tree.

Truth has many perceptions. Sickness or suffering is usually a problem of guilt in the mind, changing our perception. False perceptions produce fear. True perceptions foster love. When circumstances seem to move against us, it is because we are looking at events through our natural eyes, rather than the eyes of faith. We are unable to distinguish between advance and retreat. Some of our greatest advances we have judged as failures, and some of our deepest retreats we have evaluated as success. The insignificance of the present moment, with its seeming failures, contains within it the seeds of triumph. What seems to be may conflict with what is.

A difference in perception has been the cause of many an argument, and has been the base for most—if not all—wars. Each of the blind men in the story knew he was right, and quite a melee could have broken out had each man decided to battle for his version of what was "right." The next time you encounter a similar situation, rather than fight, ask yourself if you would rather be "right" or happy.

Faith and Perception

When we see what we want in great detail and with conviction, and it is ours. Love will enter immediately into any mind that truly wants it. When our attention is set so much upon the daily things of this world or we are engrossed in our troubles, we may be insufficiently attuned to receive instruction. We may have to receive it other ways: through other people, through circumstances, through things. Being quiet and meditating will bring us back to our inner self. The spirit cannot teach a mind that is not quiet.

What we have inside is what we project. If it were otherwise, our guilt would lie uncorrected. We must learn to see our illusions and change our attitudes through knowledge.

> "Projection makes perception.
> How we perceive a situation
> will depend on how
> we perceive ourselves. "

Fear will cause us to see the world as threatening and hostile, with anger and attack as its expressions. To begin to correct this, choose to see only good in ourselves, others, and the world. It takes practice. Begin today to love.

Never allow fear, misunderstanding and lack of forgiveness to block our way. The next time you feel angry with someone, stop for a moment, retreat to a quiet place, and see if you are also feeling some guilt. If so, choose to forgive yourself of it and let the guilt go. Learn from it and send it along its way. See then if you still feel angry. Letting go of guilt will free you to see truth rather than give you license to hurt yourself or others.

We often fight life only because we fail to perceive our own best interests. It is rare that we can know how any particular experience will fit into the whole plan for good in our lives. And often there is a difference between what we think is good for us and what really is good for us.

We eventually see that rather than letting go of people or things, we only need to let go of our attachment to them. We can physically remove ourselves from people and things; yet, if we keep mental ties to them, we probably would be better off retaining the attachments so we could learn to let them go.

So long as we seek anything, including God, outside ourselves, we will never have complete peace. All our answers must come from within ourselves. Fulfillment comes only through the real self. Negative circumstances will fail to survive when we refuse to sustain them with emotional energy.

Perception and You

We are on our life's journey. We do not have to reuse and regenerate old lessons or thoughts and perceptions. We can create new tools that serve us better.

If we call ourselves negative things, our mind and body will honor that. It will send the signal out through our bodies to create what we have thought and said. I f we want positive to expand in our lives, we must speak it, think it, and act it. We can choose to stay focused on what we are for, and not on what we are against.

It is impossible to teach by criticism. Criticism focuses on what is not. On areas that are lacking. Only by love, firmness, acceptance, and seeing the good in others can we see the good in ourselves. We must imagine perfection if we are to attain it. Perfection is a way of perceiving. Do our best each day. Be as perfect as our knowledge allows us, knowing we are already perfect, just as God created us.

It's fun to practice and see our perfection. Each time we overcome, release and forgive, we become stronger and improve our ability to imagine ourselves as perfect and joyful.

Choosing to get rid of old programming is the first step. Desire is the first and most important ingredient to healing. People who really want growth and freedom from pain come into therapy eager to let things go. They read every book they can and they make their growth and healing a priority. What is put into this effort comes back.

If we wish to grow and heal, it means self transformation will happen on all four levels: physical, emotional, mental, and spiritual. Any stress or illness will lead us on a journey of self-exploration and discovery of our real self. It will change our lives. Once we have experienced growth we will be unable to go back.

> "A mind expanded
> by a new idea
> will never return to it's
> original dimensions!"

We will continue the process of broadening perceptions, and eventually perceive beyond our normal sensory parameters.

Once my younger brother, Mont, and I were left on our own to play by a summer house tent where we were living while the construction on our house was completed.

To us it seemed like a summer-long vacation. To our parents it was a great inconvenience.

Mont and I didn't have a care in the world until one day when we were playing outside. We heard a terrible barking and howling noise. We looked up to see a large dog, foaming at the mouth, running down the hill straight toward us.

We were too young to know anything about rabies, we were just scared! We ran for the tent, tied the flap shut and crawled under the bed. The dog ran around and hit the tent over and over. The shadow of this dog growling and dripping foam from his mouth made him look twice as big as he really was. The terror of thinking we would be ripped to pieces made it seem like he would never go away!

After what seemed like a long time, Mont and I both fell asleep, crying.

Later I was to learn the dog was only there a short time before help arrived, but to our young, frightened minds, it was a very long, traumatic experience.

Many times in my life, when I was going through tremendous pain, I would remember pain is like the shadow of that mad dog. The fear makes it seem twice as big as it actually is, and it seems to last forever!

I appreciate the value of playing a little game I call "What If?" "What if" we could assume pain is an illusion or a temporary condition which is intended to send us a message? "What if" the shadow of the pain was enlarged on the tent of our thoughts? "What if" we gave it so much creative energy it seemed to stay for a long time? "What if" we decided we were safe and the pain couldn't hurt us because we understood about the nature of the shadows on the tent?

The ability to filter input from the senses through past experience is perhaps the most marvelous function built into the mind. That is, when input is received from the senses, the mind finds in the memory a similar incident from the past to compare it to so it does not have to recreate the entire image from scratch. It merely compares differences. Differences are much easier and faster to process than complete recreations.

When you walk into a room, you receive sensory input from your eyes that take in everything you see in the room. If the image of the room as you see it appears similar enough to rooms seen in past experience, you feel all is right or normal. If one of the chairs has a red rubber ball on it, however, you would notice the ball right away. Your mind would perceive that the ball does not belong there. It does not compare with your past experience with chairs. If a mouse were to run across the floor, you would notice it right away, because it is in motion while everything else is still.

The images your mind uses for comparison are stored in memory. When those images are stored in traumatic memories, they have priority over all others because those memories are associated with survival. They are also highly distorted by pain, so the filtering will become distorted.

For instance, during the trauma of the mad dog, I received a trapped false message or a neural distortion. Since I was able to cry and express it at the time it happened, I processed it or "released" it. If I talked about the incident over and over without processing it, I could do a lot of recreating of the experience and embellish it. It would grow. Then, over the years I would run the risk of enlarging it in my mind or "giving it energy."

Recognizing this tendency to create a counterfeit of what actually happened helps us understand the importance of avoiding the tendency to develop self-deception. We can greatly facilitate our own growth by avoiding attachments to distortion and letting go of addictive behaviors which are a survival mechanism.

This can only take place by quieting the mind. There is a process involved in changing the perception and old beliefs that have not worked for you. Habits must change. People generally perceive this to be difficult, but the truth is, it is very difficult to stay negative (once we get rid of old programming) because positive, whole, unconditional love is our natural spiritual state.

The Principle of Choice & Accountability

Free will works constantly in our lives as we make choices. Our lives are a mirror of our negative or our positive thoughts. Everything that happens to us is a return to us of something we have put out, whether on a conscious or unconscious level, because we needed to learn something from it.

In learning to understand this principle, it is important to remember that these principles are universal. On every level of learning we have the ability to choose. We can choose to stay in a problem, or we can choose to let it go and replace it with love. The greatest problems in our lives are our greatest teachers. They show us our issues that need to be healed.

Until we recognize our responsibility for our choices, we have no power to change the things in our lives that we don't like or that are not working for us.

It is a matter of learning to acknowledge our accountability in every situation and in every circumstance. For example, if a little boy runs out in front of our car, and we inadvertently hit him, the law of choice would say that we and the little boy created this situation to learn. We are both accountable for *our own* individual actions. It isn't about guilt, it is about experience and learning. It is vital to learn not to judge any situation in our lives, or the lives of others, because it is essential to promote learning and growth.

This is why co-dependency can be so debilitating to relationships. When we save people from the natural consequences of their actions, we take away their accountability, and therefore, the arena for their learning and growth. This will result in the process being repeated over and over again until the lesson is learned and the cycle is broken.

How to Find Peace

One of the fears that some people have about choice is that they will choose wrong. Remember that once a choice is made, consequences begin and we are always "at choice" to choose again. There are always results that come from making a choice. If we do not like the end result of a choice, then we can simply forgive ourselves and choose again.

Choices can help to focus us on what we want in our life. Knowing what we want will create a space for more choices that are compatible with our purpose. This is why it is vital to use our choice, our free will, to have a purpose for our lives.

We are always creating. The choice is ours. Choose daily to see the good in everything around us. To achieve inner peace, think inner peace. Choose to act peacefully, moment by moment. We can choose to change old programming and limiting beliefs when we no longer believe in suffering or illness. We extend and direct our faith and heal ourselves.

Choose light and enlightenment. It is joy beyond your wildest dreams. Choose to feel loved, capable and abundant. Start today with "I am what I believe I am." It is unnecessary to search for truth, for we already have it within us. It is only necessary to remove the false beliefs.

Sometimes removing the false means getting outside help, like RET processing. One may need spiritual or technical training. Others may go through self-initiated tests and challenge the weak parts of one's personality. We create from choice, on some level, our own challenges to assist us in moving to our next level of development. We must employ our choices with integrity, honesty, and love.

Consider the following:

The word "decide" comes from the Latin "to cut off" and "to separate" and "to pass judgment". According to Webster's Dictionary, it means "to bring to an end".

The word "defend" means "to fend or ward off", "to forbid or prohibit", "to resist", "to try to justify." It is an interesting human characteristic that we tend to first decide and then defend. We pass judgment, then defend our position with justification. As we decide, we take ourselves toward an end. We defend, or justify our position, and, thus solidify ourselves in the decision. We can recognize those times when we have decided by noticing how necessary we find it to defend ourselves. We only need to defend ourselves against what we perceive as dangerous to us, therefore, we may say that we approach defense from the point of fear: We defend because we feel afraid.

What would happen if we were to look at our condition from a position free of fear? Would we then feel the need to defend? Or would we feel the desire merely to observe and grow. Most of us spend much of our time reacting to and defending against perceived fears. We decide, then defend; we pass judgment, then we react. We then become the victim of our own decision and defense, giving away our power to our decision and defending our loss with justification.

This brings us to the concept of choice and commitment. To choose connotes that there are options that one can select from. Webster defines the word "choose" thus: "to exercise the power of choice". With choice, there is power. With decision there is defense. To commit, according, again to Webster, means "to entrust into the care of another", "to do", "to give in trust". It would appear from these definitions, that commitment has to do with trust, whereas defense has to do with fear. When we choose, we have the option to choose again.   When we decide, we solidify ourselves into one option to the exclusion of all others.

To decide and defend is to solidify, separate, and die. To choose and commit is to select with power, and trust life to accomplish it.   Accountability is the ability to account or bring into balance cause and effect through one's choices. With RET one has the opportunity to release the frozen thought forms created through decision and defense. This allows, in the present moment,   a new point of power through choice and commitment into accountability (balance).

The Principle of Cause & Effect

The principle of cause and effect is known by many cultures and by many names. It is called *Karma*, "What goes around comes around," "The Law of the Harvest", or "As a man soweth, so shall he reap." The concept is the same, regardless of the name. It is "Cause and Effect."

Cause and effect means that what we give out comes back to us multiplied. Actions and thoughts, negative or positive, are governed by this principle.

This principle, as all principles, works for us or against us. Therefore, it is very important to understand it. Whatever we send out will return to us multiplied. Whatever emanates in our thoughts, feelings, or actions will return multiplied many fold.

While learning this principle, I remember driving with a close friend one day. We had been discussing this principle. Suddenly, for no apparent reason, the car in the lane beside us swerved in front of us, barely missing the front fender. My companion responded to this by yelling out the window, "I'm sending you love, you #$@%&*!"

This may not be an example of fully comprehending the principle, but it was a start! At first we may not truly feel kind and benevolent towards another, but as we say it...so it will become! Begin with knowing we are love...gradually everything else in our life will reflect this belief!

Forgiveness

I learned many things about forgiveness by studying *A*

Course in Miracles. Extending forgiveness is one sure way to learn unconditional love.

The inner self speaks to us saying, "forgive and choose again. Find peace." Forgiveness is the answer to attack. Attack is deprived of its effect when answered with love. Forgiveness is the key to happiness. To achieve love, love moment by moment, and think and act lovingly with forgiveness.

Gratitude goes hand in hand with love. Where one is, the other must be found. See love in ourselves and we will see it everywhere. Let there be no effect from the cause. Choose peace.

When the wish for peace is genuine, the means for finding it is given in a form each mind that seeks for it in honesty can understand. Whatever form our lesson takes is planned for us so that if our desire for understanding is sincere, we will know. If we ask without sincerity, there is no form in which the lesson will meet with acceptance and be learned. It, therefore, must be repeated in another way, so we can choose again. To have peace, teach peace. When we have seen others as ourselves we will be released and know our worth. Only appreciation is an appropriate response to our brother. Gratitude is due him for both his loving thoughts and his need of help. Both teach us and bring love.

An exercise from *A Course in Miracles* that I like is as follows: "This week, send love thoughts to everyone. See those thoughts as beautiful rays of light emanating from and radiating outward to all. Replace all negative thoughts with these love thoughts. After a week, how do you feel?"

We create according to our beliefs. What we do on a physical level affects our higher levels. Each of the levels that we have, physical, emotional, mental, and spiritual, are effected by the other levels. When something is changed on the mental level, it filters through to the other levels. It is important to note that we are learning on all levels. Physical learning may be quite different than emotional or spiritual learning.

Through this principle of cause and effect, if you don't learn a lesson on one level, your highest self will create a way for you to learn the lesson on another level. If a lesson is not learned on the emotional level, it may manifest through a physical illness. All situations of *dis-ease* are for learning and for good.

Pain is a signal of unbalance and disharmony of energies on the physical level. On the emotional level we express fear, anger, guilt, and love. This relates to the self. On the mental level we think and learn. On the spiritual level our emotions extend beyond self and cause and effect to encompass all humanity. Our creativity shifts to universal love on a celestial level.

We must remember there are degrees of growth on each of the physical, emotional, mental, and spiritual levels. On the highest spiritual level cause and effect do not apply. On this level, there is only the effect of unconditional love!

Poet Robert Bly succinctly describes the principle of projection as it applies to cause and effect in the five stages of projection (with additional material added by us):

1. **We search for and find the perfect person to hold our projection.** For example, if we have not claimed our leadership or beauty, we may idealize someone with strong leadership skills or idolize someone who we perceive as beautiful. If we have difficulty expressing our anger, we will often experience difficulty with someone who does express anger. In this stage we never see people for who they are; we see only what we want them to be for us.

2. **The projection begins to slip.** We begin to see that our

idol may be something other than what we have projected; however, we readjust the projection with rationalization and excuses because we don't want to believe the projection is part of our own nature. For example, the effective leader may have unskillfully handled a situation, yet we rationalize that everyone has a hard day or that the people involved actually deserved the treatment. By doing this, the projection that had begun to slip is put quickly back into place.

3. **The projection totally falls off.** At this point no rationalization can be made. We are forced to see who the person is beyond what we projected. We become disappointed, angry, blaming, and judgmental. Now we have the choice to either move to stage four or to pick up the projection and look for another person to carry it for us rather than bring it home. Often we spend years just doing stages one, two, and three. We find different people to hold the same projection of those parts of ourselves that we are unwilling to bring home and claim. For example, if we find our own anger difficult to accept, we may often put it outside of ourselves, and judge or avoid it when we see it expressed in another person.

4. **Recognition.** We realize that it was a projection, and we see that it was our own material. It is the stage of grief: grief for the lost part of ourselves that has been away for so long; and grief from the recognition that we didn't see the other person for who he or she was, and now recognize the unintentional harm that we may have done in stage three.

5. **Compassion for and integration of the projection.** In this stage we have compassion for ourselves and others with similar issues. We model the quality that we once projected rather than continue to place the projection outside of ourselves. We move into a state of responsibility and begin to exercise power over the qualities and characteristics we had once projected (stage five).

The Principle of Abundance & Gratitude

The universe operates on the principle that we always receive what we believe in or want. That law is in constant operation despite our level of understanding. For us to master abundance, we must be willing, fully and freely, to express ourselves and our talents. We must notice any beliefs we have that are opposing the principle of abundance and be willing to modify them in order to have this principle work in your behalf.

To have abundance in our lives requires a willingness to recognize that it is always available. We need only to remove the blocks and open ourselves to receive it.

When we choose to make doing what we love the core experience in our life, we move into alignment with the universe. Immediately, the infinite supply of energy is made available. We begin to feel the aliveness that comes with the expression of gratitude, and these same good feelings are felt by the people we come in contact with. The people and circumstances that will support us are attracted to us.

Attraction

As we do what we love, we direct energy into the creation of high quality products and services. The people we attract are the ones who will help us by buying our products and services—and recommending them to others.

Abundance is pushed away with negative thoughts, beliefs or fears. Begin to notice the abundance we already have. By noticing what we lack, we attract an abundance of scarcity. So focus on our blessings, friends, health, food, clothes, freedom—whatever it is we want in our lives. The universe always gives whatever we ask for. Since what we think about expands, we will receive even more. If we choose to think about lack, we will have an abundance of lack!

The good news is, we can accelerate the process of bringing abundance into our lives by expressing gratitude for all we have and receive. Man is meant to have joy. Perceive everything in our lives with a positive view point.

My son-in-law gave me an example that helped him see his bills in a positive light, and helped him show gratitude for his creditors.

"As I open the mailbox each day," he said, *"I look at the letters I have received. Who are the people I hear from the most? Not my relatives or my buddies from college. Month after month, my creditors write to me. They keep track of me when I move. They're concerned about my well-being and my financial security. If they don't hear from me, they call.*

"No one else does that. Not even my brother. I think that's kind of cool."

Letting Go

To find freedom and joy in living, one has to give it all up to get it all back. That doesn't mean that we need to go out and sell off all of our possessions and then buy them back in order to become abundant. What it means is that we need to let go of our *attachment* to those possessions or relationships.

Whenever we let go of our attachment to something, it will return to us again multiplied. What we are not willing to let go of becomes a source of anxiety and threat. A relationship based upon clinging, possessiveness, or attachment will fail. There is constant worry and fear. It is only when we hold people and things lightly that we can enjoy them fully.

People come into our lives to teach us and to learn from us.

Sometimes they stay for a moment, sometimes for a lifetime. When they go, we feel bad because we cling to a picture of the past or what we think might have been. The key to happiness is to allow the person and the relationship complete freedom to evolve in the highest way for them.

Clinging never feels good. It brings hardship to the one who feels the need to possess and to the one he or she would possess. When we cling to someone in resentment, we bind ourselves to that person by our thoughts and memories.

The metaphor of seeing life as a river is an apt one. The river of life would have us flow to the ocean; instead we would rather cling to the rock upon which we dashed our foot.

It is impossible to change the events of the past. We can, however, change the way we look at those events. Those who seemed to bring us pain and hardship were our teachers who presented us with challenges that helped us to grow. Once we realize the problems were only there because of the way we perceived them, we free ourselves and them. Relationships can heal, growth can happen, love can replace fear.

It's Time to Start on Our Journey of Abundance

We all deserve abundance in our lives. An abundance of health, happiness, love, money, friends and intimacy. Look at our lives and our bodies. We've spent our lives creating both of them. It may be time to change the lesson and move on!

Lack of any kind in life is a direct message that we are not loving ourselves. Love ourselves and we will heal and change our life. It also will produce tremendous abundance in our lives. There is always abundance in the Universe. An abundance of poverty and lack, or an abundance of wealth and health.

Start seeing ourselves worthy to receive abundance, and we will become that way. See our perfection. To experience

94

total abundance in our lives we must think and feel abundance all around us, moment by moment. The past is an illusion. The future a vision. We have only this moment to make anything happen. Open ourselves to your abundance. We must select peace, joy, serenity, love. Be in alignment with life. Withhold love from no one—ourselves or others. Love governs the principle of abundance.

Some Ways to Begin

Flow With the Universe

Too often the world teaches that life is a struggle. Many times that really feels true. That is only because the way we have been taught to live goes directly against the way the universe works.

Have you ever said something like this to yourself: "I could really be a really great musician if I only had a recording contract."? The world would have us believe that we can't be something until we have the trappings that show we are that something.

According to Wally Minto's book, *Alpha Awareness,* the universe works like this:

Spiritual	*Mental/Emotional*	*Physical*
BEING ————————> DOING ————————> HAVING

The world teaches this:

Physical	*Mental/Emotional*	*Spiritual*
HAVING ————————> DOING ————————> BEING

and life becomes a struggle. So much time is spent trying to *have*, that we never get to be.

Looking at the above example in this light, first we

would *be* a musician, then you would be able to *perform* as a musician, then you would *have* the things that a great musician would have.

To put it another way, we wouldn't first build our house (create it physically), draw up plans (create it on a mental level), the decide what it will look like (create it spiritually). Instead, we have a feeling or idea of the type of house we would like, then we draw up the blueprints, and then create the house on a physical level.

The same goes for life. Just "be", leaving details to a higher power. If we can do this, it seems to work much faster. (Consider trying this if you are caught in this belief system)

Affirming The Perfect Day
The Perfect Day starts out with a good positive statement. To make your own statement, use the following example:

(Notice that each sentence includes feelings, rather than details. Use this statement at the beginning of each day and whenever you feel less than peaceful. It is a great way to expand your mind and see the joyfulness around you.)

I awake feeling grateful for the wonderful rest. (Good thoughts)

I notice a calm and peaceful feeling in my body. (Perception)

I am eager and grateful to start the day. (Abundance)

I feel centered and balanced from doing what I love. (Harmony)

I am looking forward to all the new experiences I shall have and all the love I shall give and receive. (Practicing my perfection)

I realize that everything in the universe is perfect, and only perfect things happen to me. (Negative and positive are for my growth)

I sense a direct connection to Infinite Intelligence, and trust that I will be guided perfectly as I use my intuition. (Choice and accountability)

I am filled with joy and happiness and see myself radiating that joy to everyone all day long. (Acting "as if")

Some Other Ideas

Here is a checklist of things we can do to get this principle working in our behalf:

a. Replace negative thoughts, statements and actions with positive, loving ones. Reframe thoughts that are negative. Have faith, and act as if we already have what we want.

b. Spend more time doing what we love. Express and develop our talents, and share them with others.

c. Make each day a perfect day. It is perfect when we have done our best.

d. Participate in a support system to help us develop new habits.

e. Notice what works and keep doing it.

f. Be thankful. Count your blessings. List them individually.

g. Release all attachment to illusion (things that are temporary). Since we really own nothing in this life, abundance is merely seeing we have all things already.

The Principle of Health & Healing

The idea that energy follows thought becomes readily apparent in the study of the Principle of Health and Healing. Stated simply: the mind directs the body; you direct your mind.

Recently the field of knowledge about health called *psychosomatic medicine* has experienced growth and acceptance as more people have become aware of the mind/body connection. This knowledge states that many or most of our troubles manifesting themselves as physical symptoms have their origin in mental or emotional disturbance.

All illnesses have their primary origin in the mind rather than in the body. Although a person's physical health can be imperiled by certain emotions, this concept goes beyond the physical level. All pain is due to an imbalance somewhere in your being. It is the evidence of some form of toxin. It may be toxic food, toxic emotions or a toxic relationship.

Physical pain warns that something is wrong in the body. Symptoms can include: headache, diarrhea, constipation, colds, allergy, indigestion, and weight problems.

Mental pain expresses itself in anxiety, fears and depression. Other symptoms are: over sleep, loss of work, or overwork, fear of losing what you have, stress, worry.

Emotional pain, such as a sense of loss of a loved one, insecurity or low self-esteem can manifest itself in symptoms like rejection, loneliness, anger, loss of appetite, inability to concentrate, depression, boredom, restlessness, hostility, violence, crying, guilt, and the "poor me" syndrome.

Spiritual pain manifests through closing up or resisting growth, denial, suppression or projection of blame, feeling unfulfilled, unloved, or unappreciated.

Body, mind, emotions and spirit only seem separated. This belief in separation is part of the illusion. Some imbalances that occur within our system often overlap one another. For example, have you noticed when your body is injured or ill, your mind functions poorly, too? When we are under an emotional strain, it is difficult to concentrate. If there is bickering and hatred among family members, one becomes socially sick. If spiritual appetites degenerate, one becomes morally sick. Our emotions are tied up in our attitudes.

Dr. Karl Menninger of Topeka, Kansas, stated that more people in the United States are mentally ill than are hospitalized for all other diseases and illnesses combined. That is because disease (dis-ease) has its roots in thoughts and mental attitudes.

Self-mastery is perhaps the greatest accomplishment . It is apparent when we train the mind to extend and increase authority over the body. Life is the place where we are highly rewarded for the development of the mind. We usually have great authority over our limbs. If we *will* our fingers to bend, they will obey. Our legs move merely at the suggestion of our will.

This authority has different degrees of control. We have rather complete conscious control over our fingers. Most people have little conscious control over their heart or liver. Between these extremes are all the rest of our self-control in ideas, industry, feelings, emotions, or instincts.

Our Health is Our Responsibility

What we focus on expands. Visualize our perfect healthy self—on all levels—and act as if. Having good physical, mental and spiritual health will give our spirit a better place to dwell. Our entire being acts as a unit: one aspect will fail to be completely healthy without the others.

Comfort in the body is evidence of being in alignment. On the other hand, discomfort is evidence of being out of alignment. To correct any dis-ease, whether spirit, mind or body, you must go to the source of the discomfort and correct the perception. Through being quiet (meditation and listening) the spirit will assist us in correcting the perception that is making us ill.

If we give our illness energy, it will grow. When we are angry, unforgiving, or fearful, we teach others—and strengthen in ourselves—the belief that anger, guilt, and fear are real. If we so choose, these emotions will cease to exist on earth for us.

> "It is time to wake up from
> all the illusions. View things
> from a greater height and find
> what you can do to take
> the negative energy away."

An important part of a strong physical body is a well-regulated elimination system whereby the body can discharge impurities. That is just as important to our mind and emotions as it is to our bodies. That is why it is important not to squelch or hide emotions and feelings. Rather, these things should be expressed in healthy ways. Rapid Eye Technology is one quick and effective method to discharge pent-up negativity.

Every situation, when perceived in a universal context, becomes an opportunity to heal. All healing is the release from fear and from our perceived negative past.

We heal ourselves by recognizing our own worth; we heal others by recognizing the wholeness and divinity within them. When we heal another we heal ourselves. We are made well while serving another. To forgive is to heal.

When we have seen our brothers as ourselves or learn to love our neighbors as ourselves, we will be released from being out of balance and become emotionally healthy.

Avoid Labeling and Judging

Labeling and judging are blocks to achieving healthy relationships. Prejudices kill the ability to see the healthy, whole and divine in another.

Some labels that I have overheard people use include the following:

"I can't sing, write, or dance"

"Your dress is sloppy"

"We are poor"

"You're always causing trouble"

"He is gentle"

"She is so overpowering"

"I'm so accident prone"

"He's shy"

"She is always like that"

Each of us could probably supply our own list of labels we've been given or that we give ourselves through our self-talk—even if it is only in jest. Labels tend to stay with us. We are all carrying around labels from our childhood, and many of those labels still have an impact on how we live our lives.

The following is a summary of how we label our experiences and the results of this labeling:

• We label someone or something because of what we

know or perceive from experiences, or from hearsay.

• We use this label and control or manipulate people or events to make it true.

• We disregard evidence that suggests the label is inappropriate, dismissing it as accidents or mistakes. Denial.

• The result becomes a pattern that we trust and set up.

• We expect this plan to work and create a "belief system."

• If our expectations are unfulfilled, we blame the guilty "other" who caused the failure, try to change their thinking, or get rid of them so we can be right.

You Are Always Right

Isn't it a great feeling to know that you are always right? Our thoughts are so powerful that whatever we believe in will happen. If a person chooses to believe in illness, he will have it; if a person believes in health, he will have that.

As difficult as it might be to admit it, at some level we chose our life and life situations. Whatever your situation in life, there is something there for you to learn and experience. There really is a purpose for everything. If we are not happy with the lessons we are learning, set our intention to learn the lesson quickly. If we ask, we really will receive. Then we can learn the lesson quickly and choose again; choose to be healthy and whole. All things are possible through faith.

To direct your thoughts to focus on health and healing, one tool that creates value is the use of affirmations. Affirmations are simply statements about your condition that are stated in the present and stated positively. Some examples of positive affirmations are: "I am healthy right now," "I am loved right now."

Some people have said, "I can't do affirmations. They feel like a lie because what I am saying isn't true." This is where faith enters in. One definition of faith is a hope for things unseen. That is the value of stating the affirmations in the present tense: we are not *faking* it, we are *faithing* it.

Some affirmations that I use are:
"I love and approve of myself"
"I see the divine in every situation"
"I have an abundance of all things good"
"Everything I eat turns to health and beauty"
"My actions serve the highest and greatest good"

Make your own list of affirmations that resonate for you. Look at the areas of your life that you want to have healed, or characteristics you want to develop. State them in the positive, in present tense, and focus on them daily with faith.

Affirmations are best done in a relaxed, alpha state: a quiet, meditative condition. Meditate by first finding a place in your life where you are already experiencing meditation without recognizing it. That could include times when you are daydreaming or doing repetitive tasks, such as washing dishes. Then relax and visualize things as you want them to be. Clarify in your mind what you want, and create a statement that fits appropriately like the examples above.

Meditation is a simple act. It is a good preventive medicine for stress. It is a tool for problem solving, clear thinking, relaxing, communicating with the inner child and maintaining peace of mind. When we quiet our body/mind by meditating, it provides a natural balance for the tensions that build up in our lives.

Have no preconceived expectations about meditation, because it is different for each person. It is a method to drop habits, past regrets and future expectations.

When we combine meditation with visualization it is a powerful tool for discovering our feelings then releasing those that are not working for us.

Give Thanks

Appreciate what we have. Accept ourselves as we are. Keep our sense of humor. Laugh at ourselves. Trust the seasons of life. Choose again the things we like. Practice new ways. Give up old habits and behaviors that fail to work. Touch others with music, art, writing, praise, appreciation, love, or a hand on the shoulder. Daily exercise will release chemicals in the brain that heal depression and fatigue (see *"The Ancient Secret of the Fountain of Youth"* by Peter Kelder (Harbor Press). That includes exercise on all levels, creating within us the feelings of gratitude, peace, love and healing—and a willingness to share those feelings with others.

Since our physical, mental, emotional and spiritual bodies are all connected, remember that exercising our emotions is every bit as important to our wellness as exercising our bodies. **Express ourselves!**

The Principle of Harmony & Rhythm

This principle is strikingly illustrated by placing a handful of iron filings on a thin sheet of metal and playing a certain musical note near the sheet. Wondrously, the filings will arrange themselves into a pattern. Change the musical note and the filings will rearrange themselves into another pattern. Every sound has its vibrational pattern, and the visible filings demonstrate the invisible pattern of the sound.

Our thoughts are like the sound, and the circumstances in life, like the iron filings. The filings have no volition or will of their own. They simply fall into the vibrational pattern of the sound.

In the same way, automobiles, money, food, jobs, and relationships have no particular will of their own. Their nature is to follow the direction of the waves of thoughts that we send out.

Some say, "Look what I created!" Another way that could be said is, "Look what I attracted!" The word "circumstance" neatly depicts the process: *circum* means "around;" *stance* means "stand." Circumstances are the conditions that stand around us, magnetized to us by the central core of our thought-forms. Change the thoughts at the center of the magnetic field, and we change the conditions that stand around us.

There is a basic rhythm to all God's creations—including us. We notice it when we are quiet enough to listen. Each of us has a natural rhythm. Life is simple when we hear, feel, and follow in harmony and rhythm. Meditation and visualization improve the ability to hear, feel, and become more sensitive to our inner self and the world around us. As we practice being quiet, the inner self will teach us and we will see that miracles are natural expressions of love.

Often a piece of music is called beautiful because of the interplay and harmonious synchronization of the notes. In fact, some music (such as Baroque) can actually program or format a person's brain to facilitate learning. This harmonious interplay extends beyond music for our ears. The infinite intelligence of the universe is behind the rhythm and harmony we need in our life. As we become more practiced in using these principles, we pick up the natural guidance that is there for us always, formatting a life into a divine pattern.

To increase our harmony and rhythm we can increase our understanding of the information we receive from our five basic senses: touch, sight, taste, hearing and smell. Then we can become more aware of our other senses, such as intuition and energy. When we are in harmony with these principles we draw upon the powers of nature or heaven. All is in harmony. All things work together for our good.

When we react to anger, confusion, anxiety, or fear in another person or ourselves, we encourage the other person to believe he is presenting the truth. We need only to react with love. The ideal response is to disregard the illusion the other person is expressing and see him as perfect and joyful.

We occasionally fall into the temptation to perceive ourselves unfairly treated. We can be treated unfairly only by ourselves. We are only victims of the world if we think we are. Rather than what others or the world do to us, it is what we believe they've done to us, or what we believe we've done to ourselves that make up our problems. Deprivation is the feeling we experience when we feel we are isolated or separate. We then project blame, anger, hate to others.

When we feel less than total abundance in our lives, it is only because we are pushing it away. Relax. The one thing each of us has is the potential ability to have total choice over how we feel at any given moment. We own our power when we choose how we feel or how we react. We are in alignment with the principle of harmony and rhythm when we choose unconditional love and peace.

This ability to draw conditions to us has tremendous practical implication. It means we can use our thoughts to create the life we want. It means that we can really change for the better. It means that things no longer have power over us, for we realize that they are just the manifestations of our thoughts, and nothing more.

To achieve a life that works perfectly, think perfection and see perfection in ourselves and others, moment by moment. It is possible to see the good in ourselves and in others in any circumstance and in any way of being.

Harmony and rhythm means we keep a balance physically, emotionally, mentally, and spiritually, and can operate in all levels. For instance, I have met people who are so intellectual that rather than see the beauty of the sunrise they explain the refraction of the light. Others are focused so intensely on spirituality that they can't come to earth long enough to make a living. Each level has value and importance for our learning and good. It is important to honor each level to be in balance.

This principle is perhaps best expressed in the magic of music! Music is a powerful influence in our daily lives. There are three basic ingredients of music--melody, harmony and rhythm. Melody and harmony are universal in nature. The solar system maintains its order because of the vibrations of each individual planet. They comprise a "chord" of music which is unique to our place in space.

Rhythm belongs to the earth. It is the method whereby a song is broken up into measures and notes are assigned different values of time. It is the rhythm or "beat" of a song which involuntarily sets your toe to tapping!

There is another ingredient of music which is not present in all music. But when it is present, it changes lives. Even plants and animals respond to it!

What is this fourth ingredient? It is LOVE! When music contains this element, it performs miracles! It sets into motion natural fources which begin a tumbler-like action, a turning of the tide in the lives of people.

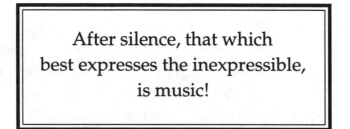

> After silence, that which
> best expresses the inexpressible,
> is music!

Research into the science of sound, or vibration, helps us understand that creating music requires the interaction between the right and left brain. In a very real sense, music transcends the mind and goes directly into the heart!

Music is an integral part of RET processing as well as the cognitive work. It can be a powerful way to access the *ability to feel* in clients who have endured so much pain that they have dissociated from life and become *"past feeling"*.

While listening to music can penetrate even the hardest heart, the activity of creating music--expressing oneself through music--develops a person's ability to organize creative thoughts and to express them effectively. It doesn't seem to matter whether that creation of music is in the form of humming a tune or in performing in a concert. Feeling will happen!

Researchers have studied Baroque music to discover why it is so powerful in assisting in learning. The combinations of notes, the patterns of the music, creates order in the brain in much the same way a computer formats a diskette to implant a grid or map which will allow information to be stored in a location where the computer will know precisely where to go to retrieve it.

Why is order so important? To create is to organize that which is unorganized. There is no judgment between order or chaos, both are necessary to the process of growth and creativity. To make use of the information we accumulate throughout our lives, we need to be able to retrieve it. If there is no order, no system for storing and retrieving that information, it is much like a file cabinet with no separate folders, just piles of "stuff". We know it's in there, but we aren't able to find it.

People with Alzheimer's disease are losing this grid pattern, this map for how to store and retrieve information. Remarkable results are being achieved with Alzheimer's patients through the use of music therapy.

An interesting phenomenon is occurring...like salmon turning upstream to spawn. The elements of the earth, the minds and hearts of the people on the planet are beginning to polarize. There is a gathering of order, a gathering of those who follow the principles which created our universe. There are multitudes of people making a choice for order.

What is left is chaos; *that which is in conflict with order*. Each person is responsible to make conscious choices about the level of vibrations by which they desire to be influenced!

When all our levels are in alignment (physical, emotional, mental and spiritual), we are "in tune". We will feel in alignment with the universe and the principle of harmony and rhythm. We have once again aligned with the "one song".

Part Three

Rapid Eye Technology - The Training

How To Become
a RET Technician

Many clients of RET become excited about the results they experience and want to share RET with their family and friends by becoming a technician themselves. RET is offered to anyone meeting the requirements. Many therapists of other models also take RET training because it discharges trauma so fast. Certification classes are scheduled through The Center in Salem, Oregon.

Once a client catches the vision of the importance of healing the inner self, they are often motivated to learn. They want to learn because they understand how their families can benefit from this new technology. There is an opportunity to share the miracle of healing thru RET with others. Once the skill is developed, the potential for healing is endless.

RET works beautifully with other models. Many professionals in the field of self-recovery find they want to add the RET model to other methods they are using because it has such powerful results. Many find it works much more quickly and effectively because it goes beyond simple awareness and actually releases the traumatic memory at the cellular level and restores trapped life-force energy to the client. Using RET will discharge the negative energy and reframe the situation to a more positive one.

Many professionals have found that after only one

session, RET will unlock blocks in a client that conventional methods were ineffective with over a period of months or even years! RET is more than therapy, it is spiritual work. It works in direct harmony with the intent of the client and restores them to a healthy clarity of mind, body, and spirit.

Requirements

The requirements for becoming a certified Rapid Eye Technician begin with the student receiving a minimum of six to twelve sessions of personal RET as a client. This also includes going through Neural Integration (bonding) and Inner Child work with RET. It is important to experience the powerful healing of RET in order to have a first-hand knowledge of the far-reaching emotional and physiological effects of the treatment. It is also important to be clear of your own issues if you expect to assist others on their healing path.

The next requirement is reading a number of texts which help to open up the cognitive awareness of the student as he expands his understanding of the various belief systems he will be encountering and also technical studies and background for RET.

Certification for the RET process consists of two six-day training sessions. The first week includes full-day sessions with instruction, demonstration and practice, and lectures and workshops. Students also get hands-on experience working as a technician with trained, certified RET staff members who portray clients.

The students return for a second week as a staff person, working with new trainees and assisting them in their learning process.

In order to staff, a person must have at least 50 hours of practice as a Rapid Eye Technician. Returning to staff helps to reinforce what they have learned and gives them a chance to practice in more detail and participate in the teaching. Staffing is an enjoyable experience; many come back several times to serve as they were served. Students may return to staff as often as they wish, to increase their confidence.

The procedure is relatively simple. Since each client processes experience differently, the student learns how to guide the client to access the trapped traumatic memories, assist them as they duplicate the emotion which releases the energy locked up in the distortion.

The student learns how to use the eye-catching device to subliminally access the various right/left brain quadrants as the client is rapidly blinking their eyes. This is more of a"hands on" learning experience as the technician has studied the technique ahead of time. It is vital that the basic pattern is administered correctly to access all the modalities, i.e., visual, auditory and kinesthetic. When the basic model is learned, then other various tools are introduced. Subsequent classes about these tools are offered to enable the technician to become more skilled.

Also taught is the importance of accessing the higher senses, which reach far beyond the limitations of the five senses to assist in healing. Students are taught to see their clients whole and healed so they are able to help their clients broaden their perception.

Students discover there is only one genuine feeling: love. It comes in numerous guises: happiness, kindness, gentleness, teachability, trust, acceptance, understanding, compassion. All other emotions are experienced because love is perceived as missing: fear, anger, jealousy, revenge, criticism, low self image, loneliness, fear of abandonment, and so forth.

The RET technician better serves their clients as they increase their ability to live healthy principles, or laws. No learning is so powerful as that which is taught by a teacher who is experiencing the benefits of the skills they are teaching about. It is essential to be a living example to those you desire to serve.

A certified technician is required to go through a recertification course once every two years after their original certification to keep current with ongoing research and new developments. It also gives them a chance to share their own experiences with others so that all may grow together.

RET Mastership (Components that accompany RET)

Beyond the certification, which allows you to practice RET, there are other levels of training that will assist you in healing work and building up your own business.

A Mastership Level course is offered. You will have further training in disciplines which support RET.

Rapid Eye Technology is continually growing, and more and more research is coming to light that explains how and why RET works. Continuing education is essential in moving you and your clients forward.

For more information about RET Mastership, contact The Center for Self Discovery, 3748 - 74th Avenue SE, Salem, Oregon 97301, or call (503) 399-1181.

Part Four

Rapid Eye Technology -
How and Why it Works

RET and the Physical, Emotional & Mental Bodies

So, how does RET affect the physical, emotional and mental bodies? Our experience over the past few years has demonstrated to us that physiological changes do occur with RET. Like REM sleep in which the body discharges through the night (leaving such things as sleep in the eyes and "morning breath", emptying the bladder, etc.), RET can affect the physical body with symptoms of discharge: halitosis, tingling, and eye condition changes. Further, because of the interconnection of all the bodies, RET often affects the overall health of the client as it did in the following case study.

Case Study

When we first met her, Joan was in intensive care and she called and asked me to come and help her. She was suffering from infection in her lower abdominal area and was not expected to live. The poisen created in her body by this infection was systematically shutting down other vital organs. The doctors had to go in and cut out a lot of her intestine and she was left with a colostomy and was unable to have normal bowel movements. She was on medications which were not helping to improve her condition. The side effects of all this different medicine was causing her to hallucinate and she was consumed with fear that she was going to die and not be able to finish raising her son.

Over a period of a couple of months, I went into the hospital every day and began teaching her to image. To see herself whole and healed. I surrounded her with my love and belief that she could be completely healed according to her faith I taught her to bring in the healing light of unconditional love that her creator had for her. She gradually was able to understand how to stay in the light and trust that her body could heal itself. She began to improve with imagery and daily Reiki treatments. The doctors were so amazed with the progress that they allowed me to be with her at any time in order to do the Reiki sessions. As she continued to improve, the doctors were convinced the change must be from some higher power. They could hardly believe the progress which she made.

When she left the hospital I continued to see her daily. When she was strong enough, we began RET in conjunction with Reiki. By the end of that year, she began having normal bowel movements which was medically impossible. She went back into surgery and they re-connected what was left of her bowels, removed the colostomy and she continues to have normal bowel movements. Thru RET, Reiki and Love, she has regained her health. We lovingly refer to Joan as our "miracle lady".

We have experienced physical improvement in health with most of our clients. Our belief is that when the emotional and mental trauma is released the body will begin to heal itself. We encourage our clients to learn a new way of perceiving their world in our "Life Skills" class.

According to Newton's first principle of motion, things in motion tend to stay in motion. We experience this truth as we observe clients who come in with addictive and compulsive behaviors. Thus, a drug addict, even though he may lose the desire behind the addiction, may still take up the habit again out of momentum alone. A person on a course of personal destruction set up by his past traumas will tend to continue on that course unless a new course is offered. It is always his journey and we honor each person's path. We simply offer a new or different way by way of education. The classes which teach new living skills are every bit as important as the release of past emotional baggage. Since energy follows thought, if our thoughts continue to be negative, we can recreate other similar negative incidents out of habit.

The systems of the body work in relation to others in a coordinated manner. Therefore, a feeling of depression (a negative emotional condition) can cause the digestive system to slow, the blood to thicken, the bones to become more brittle, the muscular system to tense up, the reproductive organs to constrict, and the urinary system to malfunction and the pupils to dilate. Fear (a negative emotional condition) can cause the heartbeat to increase, the immune system to deteriorate, the digestive system to constrict, the adrenal system to flood the body with adrenaline, and the eyes to burn.

It is the nature of our physical body to work in conjunction with our emotional body. This creates a system that serves us without our conscious attention. In other words, we do not have to think about how the physical body will react to emotional stimulus; it just does it automatically. It does it perfectly every time. That is, the body produces just the right chemicals, in just the right amount, and at just the right time to produce an appropriate (by its standards) response for the emotional stimulus.

We have found that respiratory conditions often respond to the release of negative emotional material related to the inability to speak up for oneself. Chest conditions often respond to release of negative emotional material related to sadness or grief. Headaches often respond to the release of negative emotional material related to invalidation and feelings of being not good enough.

Even though the release of negative emotional material often causes a change in physiology, we also acknowledge the value of good medical practices including, at times, surgery and other major medical procedures. Therefore, we encourage all clients to stay in close communication with their physicians when undergoing treatment for physical disorders. We do not claim any medical miracles with RET although some have occurred. We claim RET to be an effective means of stress relief.

It is in this area of anxiety and stress that we have found RET to be most effective. Releasing the emotional elements of traumatic memories allows the body to heal itself unhindered by toxic emotional reaction.

We found that the body does several things during the releasing or discharging process. It is common for the fingers and/or toes to tingle, the skin to perspire, and the breath to turn sour. Much of the trapped energy comes out through the eyes. They may burn, sting, feel gritty, dry or heavy. These are all favorable indications the technology is working!

Another method of discharge that may be less obvious is yawning. Most of us believe that yawning is a sign of boredom or inattention. Yawning, in fact, is the first sign of deep level emotional discharge and benefits the yawner greatly if he will allow the yawn to be as big as it can be (opening up the mouth fully, breathing deeply with the flow of the yawn, then exhaling fully with the yawn, perhaps even making a noise upon exhaling). A good yawn is a great stress buster.

When you yawn, we believe you are discharging

trapped energy directly connected to traumatic memories. These traumatic memories that you are relating to with your yawn are stored someplace in the bodymind hidden from conscious awareness. We believe they are very basic and primal, an automatic response mechanism.

We have found yawning during RET processing is a good indication energy is being released from a "blocked" area. Sleep time is our most significant emotional discharge time, particularly during REM sleep.

In most cultures yawning is discouraged, even suppressed. Notice the next time you yawn if you have a tendency to cover the yawn with your hand or to stifle it by holding it in. Then think about what could be happening when you do so. "Stuffing" or "stifling" emotions is a common reaction to experiences we don't have skills to process.

We believe that the very act of covering up or stifling a yawn is precisely the reason so many people are emotionally sick today: they cover up or stifle their emotional discharge paths and expressions, all seemingly in the name of being "polite".

Sighing is a breathing technique similar to yawning. In the sigh, one breathes in deeply and exhales all at once in a usually noisy manner: a "sigh of relief", so to speak. Sighing is rarely stifled and is a more subtle form of stress release. Most people will sigh when confronted with a stressful situation and will feel better for doing so.

We feel that a sigh will release emotions that are on the surface. Yawning reaches deep into the psyche and begins the deep cleansing activity necessary for releasing emotional toxins trapped at the primal level.

Stretching is also a good release for trapped emotional energy. When you feel the need to stretch, really exaggerate the stretch and see how wonderful it feels.

Effects of RET on DNA and Aging

The effect on DNA structure is as yet unknown. However, considering that the DNA is the "intelligence" of the cells, it seems reasonable to assume that distortions in neural pathways would engender recordings of some sort in the DNA of each cell. A very basic study of DNA will uncover some astounding facts about our "cell memory". In other words, we take for granted that we can inherit red hair or other traits, however, we have not considered it might be possible to hand down our fears, doubts, abuses or other traumatic memories to our children.

For example, there are nearly three billion base pairs between the "double helix" in each DNA structure. These base pairs make the DNA look like a very long ladder in a slow spiral. It is the enormous number of possible sequences in these base pairs that is the secret of the vast information carrying ability of the genetic code.

Each DNA carries its own "memory" in the structure and composition of its base pairs and length. There are many DNA structures in each chromosome and many (23 pairs in the ordinary cell) chromosomes in each cell. This makes for an abundance of DNA memory or "cell memory".

In the process of reproduction, the female cell (egg) and the male cell (sperm) each have 23 chromosomes, exactly half the number in the normal cell. In each of these chromosomes is DNA from the parent. In this way the cell memory of the parents is handed down to the children from generation to generation. Including being prone to stress, our physical parts are directly affected by the emotional, mental and spiritual parts of us. It has been our experience that this "cell memory" effect is very real in our clients.

A law of nature states that all systems tend to become more disorganized as time passes unless energy is expended to generate order. In the human this law is the basis for degeneration and death called aging. In the case of the traumatic memory or the neural distortion much of our emotional energy is tied up (or frozen) in time by our bodies. When that emotional energy is released or discharged with RET we automatically regain our "frozen" energy.

The recovery of our native energy allows us to become more "organized" thus, perhaps, reversing the degenerative effects of aging. With time we may be able to substantiate this hypothesis. At this point, however, it does seem plausible since it has been demonstrated repeatedly that people do feel more energetic overall after RET sessions.

When cells divide, an interesting mechanism is called into action that causes one cell to exactly duplicate itself into another. This process of cell division is the body's mechanism for growth and maintenance. This interesting process seems to begin in the nucleus of the cell where duplicate strands of DNA, then chromosomes, then other nucleic materials are replicated according to some mysterious pattern that mystifies science. We can see the process occur with our powerful microscopes, yet the mechanism and the system by which it occurs are yet a mystery.

It does appear, however, that DNA's brother, rDNA, plays an important role in this process. rDNA is a particular type of DNA that codes for the ribonucleic acid that is part of the ribosomes - the machines through which the genetic messages are threaded as they are translated into working proteins. In other words, the rDNA tells the DNA how to replicate. It has been found by Johnson and Strehler that the loss of this rDNA in a cell will cause the cell to cease replication. Further, Johnson and Strehler have shown that the loss of this important genetic factor is directly associated with stress, particularly long term stress.

The basic idea behind the thinking and experiments is that as cells mature, they lose their ability to reproduce exactly. They may shut off ability to read, to decode certain words. According to Strehler, *"The effect would be that all genetic messages written down in sequences that include nondecodable words could not be used to produce working parts of cells, including replacement parts."* This might explain why it is that we show signs of aging such as wrinkles, greying hair, and loss of skin tone, when at the atomic level, our bodies are no older than a few hours.

Even at the cellular level our bodies are relatively young. For example, every four days or so we receive a new layer of skin cells, a new lining of the gut every day or two, a complete transfusion of red blood cells every four months. Interestingly enough, even cells that were thought to be non-reproductive such as brain and nerve cells replicate themselves in the first ninety days of life. After which they seem to lose the ability to reproduce. This is an interesting phenomenon and science has yet to discover the reason for the change. Some say it is a time response element of the DNA, that is, the DNA "knows" when it is to replicate and when it is to stop replicating. Apparently it also knows which cells it will replicate in and which it will not!

What if it were not the DNA molecule itself that made this decision? What if it were the responsibility of the host (us) that causes this change? Could it be that it is our thinking that causes the physical body to react in this fashion? Could it be that the genetic messaging, the language of the DNA, is altered by our thought processes (Chopra 1993)? Perhaps in this molecular coding scheme trauma plays a vital role in the development of the aging process? What if it were not so much a timing mechanism built into the DNA as a significant mental/emotional event occurring within the first year of life that triggers this aging (non-replicating) process. Perhaps it is within this first year that we begin to experience stress on an emotional level and, thus cause a resultant decline in the ability of our cells to replicate?

Could it be that the effect of stress, then, is a gradual loss of cell replication ability? If so, then the conclusion might be that the effect of long term stress would be aging followed by death. This may sound a little obvious to you, however, it is significant to know that the root of this aging process is just now becoming known to science.

Trauma induced distorted memories in the unconsciousness (including the coded memories in the genetic material), cause distorted perception and irrational behavior in the present time. These memories include our basic beliefs and survival instincts. They effect our emotions and our self esteem.

These memories can limit our choices at an unconscious level. The ability to act rationally becomes diminished. Potential for self-development becomes restricted. Stress becomes detrimental.

Emotional Trauma that respond to the RET process:
Feelings of Abandonment/Rejection
Addictive, Compulsive Behavior
Adult **C**hildren **O**f **A**lcoholics
Anger
Trauma of Auto crashes
Birth trauma
Codependency
Delayed Shock
Depression
Dysfunctional Family Behaviors
Emotional, Physical or Sexual Abuse

Fear
Grief
Guilt/Shame
Post-Trauma Stress Disorder
Stress/Anxiety

The traumatic memory is an emotional snowball of jumbled up emotional decisions made at the time of trauma and returned to us in present time by the restimulation of a similar incident. When we feel that the original trauma is returning to us, we tend to react similarly to survive the original experience once again - after all, we survived the first time! It is an amazing system for survival and protection of the organism. The actions and emotions that we survived with in the original traumatic incident or significant emotional event, are automatically called upon to duplicate the feat and deliver us from the real or imagined present danger. The subconscious mind makes no judgment between what is real and what is imagined. Whatever you think it is, it is!

Even though we may refer to fear as a "negative emotional condition", fear can be a wonderful protective device for us if it is used correctly. That is, when there is actual danger presenting itself. For example, it is appropriate for one to feel fear when he is standing on the railroad tracks while a train is bearing down upon him at a high rate of speed. The instinct of fear might energize him sufficiently to remove his body from the dangerous tracks in time to save his life. This is an appropriate use of the fear emotion. All the physical elements - muscles, chemicals, senses, and nerves used to cause the body to escape the train during this time of fear will be automatically called into action the next time the fear/train incident appears.

It is the *inappropriate* use of this mechanism that causes

so much trauma. Illness is a necessary adaptation of the body to the misuse we give fear by having a constant inner stress through false feelings of emergency. Because of constant anxiety, our bodies are continually being mobilized to either fight or run! The "stress juices" become toxic poisons and must be used up, neutralized or stored in the way our particular bodies can adapt. When our tissues become weak and abused, it weakens our immune system and we invite great hordes of microscopic invaders. However, a truly healthy, physical body can handle any invasion if it is not fouled with toxins and bound with tension. When a person awakens to the knowledge that his body is totally normal for this time and place, he can begin to experience life functions more freely.

It is thought, rather than time, that makes men and women age. It is all those times we thought we were in danger and were being "tricked" by our perception. All those anxiety attacks, times of panic, and fits of anger, have taken their tolls on our bodies as well as our emotional well being. For more information, read *Ageless Body, Timeless Mind*, by Deepak Chopra.

Case Study

Marcie is a 39 year old woman who stated that her problems started shortly after her divorce. She had been living in fear and panic since her husband had received custody of their three children. She stated that she was making mistakes at work and began hesitating in her decision making. She was afraid to take action on a decision because she feared doing the wrong thing. She could not afford to lose her job because of the child support she had to pay.

Marcie's incapacitating fears were interfering with her work, her relationships with her family and her resentful boyfriend. She was terrified to be in a group of people because she feared doing something wrong and being judged. She would stay awake at night reviewing things over and over. She felt tense, nervous, irritated and easily distracted. She complained of headaches, annoying body pains, and a constant feeling of fatigue. She described feelings of inadequacy, panic attacks and anger about losing her children.

It took twelve sessions of RET with Marcie (going through the inner child stages) before she felt she had her emotions under control. Her body pains subsided to a level of insignificance, her anxiety and panic attacks are gone, and she is attending life skills classes to learn new methods of approaching life. Traumatic memories began lifting in layers, each one being processed and released as it came up. Once the underlying cause of the emotional aberration was discovered and released, the physical pain left as well. Marcie's case is indicative of hundreds of cases involving stress related anxiety and panic attacks successfully treated with RET.

Case Study

Amy is 25 and the mother of three. Her mother literally carried her into The Center. She was suffering from debilitating fatigue and anxiety. She could say only a few words before she felt too tired to speak. Her mother related that she had been deteriorating physically for the past three months since a serious car crash in which she was only negligibly injured. She had been spending more and more time in bed with various infections and colds, fevers, flu, aches and pains, and general fatigue. Her monthly periods had become erratic or nonexistent.

During that initial RET session, we discovered that she had never been treated for shock at the hospital. She was "checked and released the same night." She spent nearly the entire first session working on the emotional trauma of the car crash and the resulting shock. After one session of RET she was able to walk to her car, drive home, and return to work the next day. Because of the great success of her first visit, Amy has returned for several sessions to work on other issues.

The Change in Emotions

One discharge pattern often neglected is in the change of emotions. When we change our emotional state, we experience a discharge of the previous emotional state. For example, one way of changing from one state to another would be to suddenly switch from one thought to another. When working with a client who seems to be "stuck" in a traumatic memory, the technician may suddenly ask "tell me about your grandchild".

Simply changing state will cause us to release emotional energy. When we are engaged in RET we often notice a general change in appearance when the emotional state changes. The skin tone will become clearer and the eyes will brighten. The client will often report feeling an increase in overall energy and well being as we reframe a negative emotional into a positive one.

Case Study

Jerry is a twenty-four year old man who was recently married and really looking forward to becoming a first time father. He had a good job as a computer programmer, and life seemed to be going well until his wife suffered a miscarriage. This trauma flipped Jerry into another state.

Suddenly, Jerry's life began falling apart! He lost his job, had his arm broken in an auto accident, and began having relationship problems with his wife and parents. He had to be medicated for the pain in his arm. Jerry came in for RET sessions which were able to allow him to release the present pain which was attached to childhood trauma.

The rapid return to a peaceful state encouraged Jerry to continue RET sessions to assist him in a deeper understanding of his healing process.

Performing RET for Another Person

Can one person do RET work for another? If you could do RET for someone else, why would you want to? How could you tell if you were clearing your own stuff, or someone elses? Would it matter? We wondered about these questions. We understood from our research into quantum physics that all molecules are connected in a kind of "quantum soup" and one entity could not be affected without it being evidenced by all other entities in some manner.

We began to understand that the generations before now never really addressed "issues" per se. They were very much into survival level existence. Their "gift" to us was to contribute to the ongoing progress of civilization...to bring us to our current state of advanced learning where we would have the luxury of contemplating our "issues" rather than remaining on a survival level.

Perhaps our "gift" to them would be to develop a technology for healing which would finally assist is processing and releasing the trapped energy which is passed through some "emotional" DNA.

In fact, it would be impossible to heal ourselves without it affecting them as well. This healing would reach backward to our ancestors and forward to our descendants! Where we could not actually "live" their experiences, we were the literal effect of the emotions which were trapped around those experiences. Until we heal the traumatic memory it will continue to effect our children and our children's children by virtue of the fact that we continue to inflict the same traumatic memories from one generation to another.

The more we thought about it, the more we realized that could be an explanation for many unusual occurrences which we experienced with numerous clients. As a result of these occurrences, we began researching what others had found on the subject of vicarious healing, or what we call "proxy" work.

We have hundreds of cases where this phenomenon of working on behalf of another has resulted in a significant improvement in the intended recipient. What a boon to humanity! If this is really feasible, then the possibilities are unlimited for emotional healing on a rather large scale. Unwilling husbands could be helped by willing wives. Angry teens could be helped by caring parents or siblings. Hurting persons anywhere could be assisted by persons who were willing to be proxies through the instrumentality of RET. The possibilities are indeed unlimited.

It is important to remember that each persons' free agency is honored. If a person chooses not to receive the proxy work which is done in their behalf, the healing energy will not be received. However, we believe the energy is "held in reserve" until such time as they are receptive to it. Similar to prayer energy.

Obviously there is much we do not understand about our own bodymind systems. We all have heard stories of incredible acts of physical prowess by those with very limited physical strength. Perhaps it is not so much the release of energetic chemicals in the physical body that cause these displays of superhuman physical strength, as the release of mental blocks to our natural abilities? And what about those stories of superhuman psychic phenomenon such as psychokinesis and other parapsycological phenomena?

"Let me tell you something," confides Larry Dossey,

M.D., cochairman of the Panel on Mind/Body Interventions at the National Institutes of Health (NIH), *"If we ignore issues of consciousness, it'll be the ruin of alternative medicine. It could wind up just being something used as ruthlessly as synthetic drugs or stainless steel scalpels. In my opinion, the most important research activity in the entire field will be the investigation of nonlocal manifestations of consciousness."*

Nonlocal manifestations of consciousness? (This is another term for the same process we call **"proxy work"**.) The panel's report explains: "studies in mental and spiritual healing show that the mind can somehow bring about changes in faraway physical bodies, even when the distant person is shielded from all known sensory and electromagnetic influences. These events, replicated by careful observers under laboratory conditions, strongly suggest that there is some aspect of the psyche that is unconfinable to points in space, such as brain or body, or to points in time, as in the present moment."

Just what does it mean "nonlocal manifestations of consciousness?" How is it that you can do significant emotional work for someone else? Studies by respected researchers in the field of human consciousness are beginning now to substantiate claims made long ago by shamans and healers that we are all interconnected in such a way that what we do for one we do for all (see *Psychology Today, October 1993).*

In RET we can do significant work for another person by simply applying the principle of intent to the technique of RET. To us it is no real mystery. It has been done so often that we feel it is now simple fact.

Hundreds of proxy experiences have been logged over the years we have been developing the current model of RET. This principle of proxy is so powerful and so reliable that we find it useful in a number of significant applications. Angry or reluctant teenagers often can open up and find emotional (and glandular) relief through the skillful application of proxy. There are groups of RET therapists who do proxy on a regular basis as a service to mankind. The Center offers a place for such work to be done thereby adding to our knowledge of this interesting phenomenon.

Researchers in this field of RET and proxy have found that a proxy session of RET can be done rather quickly and effectively using new techniques discovered by these researchers. The body of information leading us to a new model of proxy technology based upon the principle of intent and the technique of RET is ever increasing. We have come a long way in our understanding and application of this marvelous gift.

We have also found that the most significant and profound changes of state have occurred within families. We call this generational RET, that is, processing done for the entire family back as many generations as the traumatic memories exist. Yes, one can do RET for those who have passed on. "So what does that have to do with me?" you say. Plenty!

Within our DNA are the memory traces, physical and emotional traits, and mental ties to family who have preceded us in time (Mednick 1985). It is significant to note that this DNA trace through our ancestral background provides us with substantial emotional material for work with RET. It seems that the more powerful the significant emotional event in our parents lives, the stronger that event plays a part in our current lives. In other words, the RET we do for our ancestors is RET we do for ourselves on a very deep level. We have found substantial evidence to support the idea that our ancestors are a meaningful resource for us in the release of present time emotional stress.

Woolger and others contend that the release of emotional elements from these ancestors (and others) is a worthwhile pursuit in that it often provides the client with significant connections that further the process of healing. Whether an ancestor is living or has passed on, his or her DNA traces live on in the bodyminds of their posterity. Truly, we cannot be healed without our ancestors.

Proxy Work

Case Study (personal proxy account of a student/client)

As I've spent the past several years learning and growing with the development of RET, I have come to have a powerful belief in the principle of allowing my body to be a conduit for healing energy.

Of course, it began with the desire to heal my own pain, which is an ongoing process as I experience different levels of awareness. I realized I had years of toxic emotions packed away in every nook and cranny of my physical body. I often prided myself in being physically very strong. I was seldom ever sick enough to even take a day off work. What I didn't realize is how a person can adapt to the symptoms of toxins in their system and consider themselves to feel "fine...really!". In the past few years, I've come to understand there is a great deal of difference between feeling "fine...really!" and experiencing the thrill of unbounded energy coursing through every molecule of your body!

In the beginning, it never occurred to me that I could effect a healing in anyone but myself. All I really knew was that I had an intense desire to learn new living skills and to be well! It was an internal mantra--- a chant that echoed in my ears with every waking moment: "I want to heal!" "I Want To HEAL!!" It was a personal commitment!

In my efforts to heal, I worked on "the need to release control" issues. After spending much of my life feeling controlled by others

133

and countering it with the need to control, I was finally aware I was to be concerned only with my own lessons. I became content to allow other people to learn theirs.

A wonderful side benefit of clearing toxins through RET and learning new living skills is your increased awareness of when you have "let go" of an old toxic experience. You can begin to sense when there is no more trapped energy surrounding it. You feel free. You feel released from the reoccurrence of emotional trauma about that experience.

After having the opportunity of using RET to discharge a number of childhood traumas, I noticed that occasionally I was feeling "energy" around issues which I knew I had already processed. At first I wondered if RET was only a temporary release technique. But the more I meditated about what I was experiencing, the more I began to sense that I wasn't feeling MY stuff anymore, I was feeling stuff that was coming from someplace ...or someone... else!

Then one day, in the midst of a training session with Ranae and my husband, Frank, we experienced a profound awareness. While I was in the alpha state, words began coming from my mouth which did not originate in my own mind. I was completely aware of the communication that was occurring and was excited to receive the instruction that was pouring forth. I could feel the sound flowing through my vocal chords, although I was making no effort for them to do so.

Many wonderful concepts about the work of RET were opened to our understanding. One statement in particular was very direct. We were told we were regulating many energies and that it was important for us to release control and allow the process to occur. We were told there was no urgency and the only thing which would prevent the flow of energy would be our anxiety about the process itself.

Some time after that experience, while in another healing session, I had a vivid visualization opened to my mind which left me *in tears as I came to more fully understand what "regulating many energies" meant. I was in the process of doing some deep breathing to begin moving the energy in my body; to oxygenate each cell in order to allow it to prepare to release any energy which might be trapped there.*

With my physical eyes closed, I gradually "saw" a large room with doors at opposite ends. Through one door, people came into the room while the other door allowed them to leave. I sensed the people entering the room were coming from a thick darkness. Their faces, their bodies, were drooping and lethargic. There was a "turnstile" mechanism a few feet away from the door which allowed people to leave the room and enter into the light. There seemed to be an intensity about their desire to go through the turnstile and into the light.

I became aware that the activity in the room was directly connected to my breathing. When I breathed in...the room filled with people. When I breathed out, the people went through the turnstile and into the light. As they went through the turnstile, their bodies were renewed! Their faces filled with light and they were shouting for joy! I began to weep as I realized what was happening. I started breathing in more and more deeply. I wanted each "in" breath to last longer so more people could flood into the room. I wanted each "out" breath to last longer so more people could get through the turnstile. Each breath allowed more and more people to enter into the light. For a moment I was totally engulfed in the joy of this new found awareness of what was happening!

Suddenly I felt an overwhelming sense of sadness and burden as I realized how heavy this was...this responsibility to be a "regulator of many energies". What if I wasn't willing to make this commitment for others? What if I wasn't healed enough to continue? What if...

Just as suddenly came a wave of love and light as I became aware of the meaning of the other instruction I had also previously

135

received. I remembered I was told "...there was no urgency and the only thing which would prevent the flow of energy would be my anxiety about the process itself."

A wonderful peace filled my being as I understood it wasn't my responsibility to "save" all these people. That was occurring through a power much greater than I. It was occurring through the Power of Love. My only responsibility was to be peaceful and allow my body to be used for the process. With this understanding, I felt my entire body relax.

Now, whenever I experience pain in my body, I quickly assess whether it is my pain (and many times it is, because I'm still healing) or pain I have already personally released. It is a fleeting symbol of the energy I am processing for others as they pass through the turnstile and into the light. As I remember, I just smile because I know more souls are passing through the turnstile. In the most sacred sense of the word, I have come to think of myself as a "proxy". I am filled with gratitude for the privilege.

Through the years I have witnessed the power of proxy work in my family. At first I was the only one in my family who was involved in RET. After many proxy sessions for my extended family, I now enjoy the association in RET of three brothers, a sister, a sister-in-law, a niece, both my sons and their families, including my beautiful young grandchildren. It is wonderful listening as my 5 year old grand daughter instructs her little sister who has just fallen and scraped her knee to "gather up the owie, turn it into love bubbles and blow it away!" It is so rewarding to view the efforts of my loved ones as they invest effort in their own healing. And just as rewarding as seeing the healing of my descendents, somehow, I just know my father and mother, who left this life without the understanding of how to process their pain, are also benefitting from this miracle of healing!

In RET we completely believe in the "onesong" of life and in the connection of all souls in the universe. Whether in this dimension or another, there is no separation. Not in the need to heal, not in the process of healing, nor in the results of healing.

When your intent is to heal and the power you call upon is Love, you do not need to be completely healed yourself before you can become a Bridge of Love to process the energy of others by proxy. All you need to be...is willing. You cannot effect healing in anyone who does not desire to heal...but that healing life force will remain in their energy until they are ready to receive it. We believe once dark energy is transformed by love and sent into the light, that energy will never again be used for darkness. It is in this manner that our beautiful planet, as well as its inhabitants, can be cleansed of all the darkness and pain and brought into the Light of Love. This belief is constantly reinforced by the knowledge that God is Love.

The Earth, plants and animals are natural conductors of love and light. Music is a river of vibration which penetrates the most dense darkness and carries the healing Power of Love into the hearts of all creatures.

To all of you who have discovered this "Proxy-ability" within your being, I dedicate this poem:

PROXY

Breathing...
slow...
and
deep...

Clearing my Mind...
Releasing all Fear
of this Dimension...

Preparing my Energy
To flow into all generations
Filled with unprocessed experience.

Identifying the Intent..."To Heal"
Recognizing the Power..."Love"

Wanting to remove my shoes
as I walk on the Sacred Ground
of their Pain.

Knowing with every breath I take
I am fulfilling a Covenant
Entered into so long ago...
to Give the Gift.

Allowing my Body to
Become a Vessel of Light,
A Bridge of Love.

Linking the Hearts of the Fathers
to the Children...
the Hearts of the Children
to the Fathers...

According to the Word.

Sonja Lorrigan Redford

Case Study *(Proxy - helping another)*

In Amanda's case, school was an issue buried beneath her perceived hatred for her parents. Amanda was 14 and equated parental authority with school authorities, police authorities, all adult authorities. She found it difficult to do RET because her technician represented adult authority to her. In session she was completely belligerent and uncooperative. It became apparent that she was blocking attempts to reach her. We have discovered the importance of honoring each persons desire (and *lack* of desire) to seek out their own healing journey.

This is one situation where we have had amazing success performing proxy sessions. Many times the love energy which is generated by this work will penetrate the dark energy which seems to build a fortress around a person in pain and they find their resistance softening. We found the key to working with Amanda was to first work with her parents to clear away their anxiety and need to control. Once they were able to come from a place of unconditional acceptance for her, we had her parents do proxy sessions for Amanda.

After the second proxy session with her mother, Amanda expressed a desire herself to become involved with the RET process. The progress was slow at first while we were building a foundation of trust with her. One day we asked her if she would like to do a proxy session for her brother who had recently become emotionally upset.

From the very beginning of this session, Amanda began processing deep emotional trauma and became completely cooperative. Her progress was phenomenal! She cleared up tremendous amounts of her own negative emotional stuff while imagining she was in the personality of her brother. This is possible because we are all connected by fields of energy. (If you question this, notice how uncomfortable you feel the next time you are in the presence of someone who is "acting out" negative energy!)

Suddenly, Amanda's school work became easier for her. She found herself able and willing to communicate with her parents and other adult figures in her life. It has been over three years since her first session. She has taken the RET training and has a substantial clientele. She works primarily with other young people as well as with adults. RET literally turned her perceptions around. She now feels a close bond with her parents who have continued to be involved with RET.

RET and Self Esteem

Low self esteem has been shown to be the cause of abusive relationships, family dysfunction, job stress, and distressed marriages. It accounts for most of the personal dis-ease we experience in this life. RET and the classes associated with it have proven immensely effective in this area. Once the false trapped messages have been released and reframed (changed to positive), the classwork offers the client a new sense of self worth and an increased desire for life.

Case Study

Sally, a young wife and mother, was experiencing severe depression that came on suddenly for no apparent reason. She was unable to care for her newborn, and became fatigued, listless, and very sad. Her husband was a successful lawyer. She had a beautiful new home and four healthy, happy, well-adjusted children. She and her husband are very well respected in their community contributing to many service organizations, and are involved in PTA and church activities. Sally is well educated and works according to her own schedule. Suddenly, after the birth of her fourth child, she began experiencing severe depression. Her family suggested she see a physician to get anti-depressant drugs. She resisted the idea.

Sally grew up in what she terms "an ideal family." She

was the youngest of four children. She and her siblings have always been close and remain so today. Her parents are supportive.

Sally began RET dealing with birth issues in treatment for postpartum depression. The interesting part of Sally's treatment was what she did with the information she received during session. Sally chose to share her RET session experience with her mother who disclosed that the sadness Sally had experienced while she was being born had to do with the information her mother had received at the time of Sally's birth (this was information Sally found out in an RET session and it was later confirmed by her mother):

Sally's mother had just discovered she was adopted! This revelation at the time of Sally's birth was very traumatic and sent Sally's mother into a tailspin of depression and sadness that the newborn infant took into her psyche as her own. This intense sadness and depression were later triggered in Sally by the birth circumstances of her own fourth child. Sally has recov-ered completely from her depression and has returned to her normally productive, loving life.

She took the RET training herself and returned home where her first client was her own mother! See *"Babies Remember Their Birth"*, Chamberland.

Sally's case is representative of many cases of depression. Depression is epidemic in America and many civilized nations. The effect of RET on depression is impressive. We have been especially gratified by the results of RET on this insidious destroyer of self image. The ultimate result of an unchecked depression is often suicide.

The result of RET on suicidal clients has really been exciting. We have had remarkable cases of complete recovery after near suicide. Sally may have reached that point, too, had it not been for RET.

Case Study

Mandy called late one night, at the insistence of her sister, Sharon, who had received two sessions of RET for her own fears and depression. Mandy was talking about suicide because she "could not hold onto a job, a boyfriend, anything," she said. She sounded serious, though we learn to take threats of suicide seriously no matter how it sounds (even in jest).

Over the phone, I told her to find two points on the wall in front of her that she could look at that would cause her to move her eyes from side to side as I would instruct her.

This exercise is what we call "emergency processing." It seems to gets left brain talking to right brain. Left brain asks the questions and right brain (seeing the whole picture) answers. Sometimes this solves the problem and reduces the trauma.

After a few minutes she said she was feeling better and could make it through the night. I saw her the very next morning. She said she felt foolish for calling me, yet we proceeded with a full session of RET. Mandy's connection was to her birth where her mother was told by the doctor to "hold on, hold on, not yet...hold on." while her mother screamed, "I can't hold on! I can't hold on anymore."

When Mandy discovered this important piece of personal information and realized how it was connected to her ongoing feelings of "not being able to hold on", she was elated! With RET the emotional trauma was released and the information came freely to her. She has changed completely, lost some weight that she could not diet away (she would always lose her hold on the diet), and has held onto a meaningful job for the last year.

Mandy illustrates well the concept of connection. Once Mandy could make the connection between her birth trauma decision about life: "I can't hold on anymore" to her present life condition: "I can't hold onto a job, a boyfriend, anything" she was empowered to change her condition. The ability to make these healing connections is made powerful by RET that releases the emotional element that often blocks the connection process by hiding the underlying traumatic memory. Mandy made her connections and healing because she was relieved of the emotional bulwark that kept this awareness secret.

The quick results that RET have with most suicidal clients make it a powerful tool in the preservation of life in this instance. In some cases, suicide is avoided because the root cause is discovered in session before the client gets to that point. In other words, the most effective process for clients with suicidal tendencies is prevention!

Had we had Mandy in for RET earlier when she first began feeling the depression, we may have prevented the suicidal desires. Our classes in living skills have also proven valuable in teaching new thought patterns and preventing suicide, especially in teens.

Case Study

June was having grave difficulty in her relationships and was unable to keep a boyfriend long enough to even call one a relationship. She felt fear when she was in the company of a man. She had heard of RET through a friend and attended one of the free life skills classes with her friend and her friend's RET technician. During one RET session, she discovered an early childhood rape by a male babysitter. She was reliving her rape every time she dated a man, finding herself terrorized by her dates.

In another one of her sessions, June was able to release the rape trauma and reframe her life allowing her to enjoy her dates free of fear.   She continued her RET sessions for other issues and the living skills classes to forge a new pattern for herself.   She is now in college and dating freely and has a wonderful relationship with a special man.

RET and Post Trauma Stress Disorder

Rape, Post Trauma Stress Disorder, and delayed stress syndrome are all highly responsive to RET.   June's case illustrates the effectiveness of RET on childhood abuse; even when the abuse has been hidden for years.   Among those who have felt the result of intense fear experiences, Vietnam War veterans have received quite a bit of publicity over what has been termed "Delayed Stress Syndrome" and "Post Trauma Stress Disorder".

The basic course of this type of stress is that the initial stressful incident is so intense for so long that the mind shuts it off until much later.   The veteran finds himself acting out some bizarre behavior without any understanding of the cause of the behavior.   Some break out in tears and are unable to stop.   Others find themselves suddenly confronted by an acute case of paranoia.   Each session a client has, he feels lighter and less stressful.   RET works wonderfully and quickly for combat PTSD and sex abuse.

RET and Weight Loss

Case Study

Susan demonstrates another interesting at the workings of RET.   For years Susan had been in a constant battle of the bulge.   She was seriously overweight and seemed to be perpetually on an ineffective diet program.   She had tried exercising, herbal dieting, milkshake diets, celebrity diets, and exercise machines.   She had been working with a hypnotherapist with some success, yet, as soon as the weight was off, the weight came back. She said, "I feel like a fat roller coaster."

Susan came to RET for relief of anxiety attacks that had plagued her. She discovered in one of her RET sessions that as a child she was the victim of Ritualistic Satanic Cult Abuse. Her case became very intense indeed and over the period of sessions, she released the traumatic memories of years of severe abuse and near death experiences. Gradually, Susan could release the weight with her diets and exercise programs. In other words, RET opened the door to making the weight loss programs effective.

She has lost over 100 pounds and has kept it off for over a year. We do not claim that RET will help you lose weight, however, it could release the reason for the ineffectiveness of the weight loss programs, thus opening up the avenue for change Her life, her marriage and her career are like a miracle since the effects of the sexual abuse, as well as the weight, are gone.

RET and Drug Addiction

Case Study

Raul was involved in a $100 a day cocaine habit that had developed out of an addiction to a prescription drug after an injury from a car wreck. He was often in pain and felt the need for something to make him feel "right". He knew he was hooked and could see how the cocaine was effecting his work, his marriage, and his self esteem. Besides the guilt he felt, there was a deep underlying feeling of worthlessness that was spiraling down into depression. He had a sense of helplessness that was consuming him.

His wife, Maria, had received four sessions of RET and

convinced him to try it. In his first session, Raul found that he liked the light and sound technology that was offered with the RET and was able to let go of the cocaine rather easily (it surprised him how easily he could stop). The RET assisted him in releasing the negative emotions associated with the addiction, the light and sound technology gave him a drugless replacement for the "high" he felt he needed, and the life skills classes helped him change his beliefs and behaviors that had kept him involved with the cocaine.

We have found that drug addiction is extremely difficult to overcome while the client is involved with the drug. Ordinarily, we refuse to accept a client until he/she has dried out in another program. RET will allow him/her to lose the emotional dependence on the substance or behavior, thus making the other program much more effective and long lasting. Just like Susan's weight loss program, Raul was successful because RET made his other programs more effective. In Raul's case, the light and sound technology was additionally helpful.

RET and the Multiple Personality

Case Study

We have had the privilege of working with several "multiple personality" types.   Of these, PJ is representative. She is a 40 year old mother of three. She has been married over 20 years and at the time she came in for RET she was experiencing marital difficulties. She weighed 330 pounds and felt afraid of everything.   She had been seeing a psychologist and he had diagnosed her as having multiple personalities. Her psychologist told her that it would take her about eleven years to integrate and become one person again. In 1992 she was referred to a RET technician.

PJ reported that she often lost time, losing all memory of incidents and places. Large blocks of her life seemed to be inaccessible to recall. She kept lists to remind her of everything. When she was diagnosed multiple, she started to notice the personalities within her and give them names. She came to refer to herself as "PJ and Company." She would experience a different reality with each personality that appeared. Sometimes she was suicidal, sometimes sexually provocative, sometimes she could not stand to be touched. Her family was becoming increasingly confused with her behavior. PJ reported that she had a traumatic and incestuous childhood. Her personalities protected and assisted her in her times of need. They all performed a very necessary survival function for PJ.

PJ's RET session began by relieving her present day stress. Time was spent getting to know each personality individually. Rapport was constantly being developed, and unconditional love expressed no matter which personality or issue emerged. RET was coupled with hypnotherapy and NLP techniques to bring similar personalities together so some of PJ's switching personalities would stop.

PJ was not sure if she wanted to integrate all her personalities because they served useful purposes in assisting her to cope with life. Many of the individual personalities expressed fear of integration, because if they felt that if they integrated they would die.

As processing progressed, capable, dominant personalities were put in charge of younger, less capable and some suicidal personalities. Almost a year after beginning RET, three major personalities came together and all the little girl personalities joined. PJ began to become co-conscious and her time lapses ceased. Her personalities began to take care of each other.

The little children personalities were given treats, listened to, read to, played with, and loved. A time came when the personalities began changing their names. Baby Hippo changed her name to Illusion and PJ began to lose weight. Rage changed his name to Protector.

PJ had a strong commitment to healing. She faithfully attended the free living skills classes and made major changes in her life. She began to incorporate the living skills in her family and social life. In the classes she met other people who provided new role models to grow from. She learned how to relate to men and women on a positive basis without fear. She realized that she had the strength and ability to heal.

As her family began to notice her progress, they also became interested in RET. PJ's father, mother, husband, all her children, and many members of her extended family received assistance from PJ herself and her RET technician.

It took one year of intense RET and class work for PJ to get her major personalities to integrate, and her life to become functional. She has also begun attending church services for the first time in fifteen years. PJ is continuing in RET and wants to assist other people like herself to heal. She has now taken the RET training and is working with her own clientele.

RET and Compulsive Anger Behaviors

Case Study

Johnny is eleven. He was experiencing episodes of anger at home and at school. His mother said she had tried many other therapies before calling a RET technician. Johnny's mother was concerned about putting him on medication. His behavior seemed to coincide with the departure of his father. He seemed to feel he needed to protect and defend his mother, developing a strong attachment to her. His attachment grew so fearful and so intense that he appeared to hate and despise his mother for showing what he thought was too much attention to his siblings.

Rapport and RET worked the best with Johnny. In his first session Johnny flew into a fit of rage, screaming and kicking and throwing his body around the room. His mother and I held him fast and yelled and screamed with him, encouraging him to yell it out louder and louder, all the while telling him how much we loved him. Gradually his anger seemed to drain away and we were able to begin RET sessions with him.

As we continued to work with him, whenever he would begin to act out anger, we repeated the same pattern of restraining him and matching rapport by yelling and screaming with him. Eventually, Johnny lost his need to act out in anger and so has had no more episodes of anger. We worked with his whole family until the dynamic of the system released all the underlying anger and fear. The single-parent family system Johnny participates in is well on its way to completeness and healing.

The effect of RET on compulsive anger behaviors has made it a viable alternative to drug treatments or hypnosis. The anger is simply a fearful response to environmental stress and RET is especially suited to stress relief.

RET and Teens

Case Study

When Shawn was fifteen, she was having difficulty in her high school. She was often afraid of her teachers and some of the students. Her grades were failing and she was considering dropping out of school, although she feared what her parents would do if she dropped out. Shawn received two sessions of RET before she was ready to let go of the fear and anxiety about her experience at school.

The first session was spent primarily in building rapport with her so she could trust her RET technician. The results of her sessions seemed to be immediate: she quickly noticed improvement in her grades and began enjoying school again. Her relationship with her parents improved, although she still required more work in this area. Her parents were invited to work with the technician and they agreed to get involved as well in RET sessions of their own. The greatest improvement with Shawn came when her parents were willing to get involved, creating a common goal to heal.

When a family comes in to us for treatment of an out-of-control youth, we suggest RET for the entire family unit because of the great success we have experienced in working with family systems. The stress is shared by the family as a whole and will be best treated as a family unit. Dysfunctional relationships foster codependent behaviors which create destructive behavior cycles.

The cycle continues and escalates until the family is faced with a crisis (or crises) so severe that it seems the only "way out" is to go outside for help. The alternative to this is when the family members believe that the only way to avoid the stressful emotions is to "stuff it". Of course, we realize through our experiences that "not dealing with a problem" does not make it go away, it will merely surface at a later time, usually with even more severity.

With RET these hurtful issues can effectively be addressed and processed so the family system can deal with adeloscent issues in a more appropriate and a much less painful manner. When family members are willing to do proxy sessions for other family members, they begin to feel more empathy and understanding toward those other members.

This presents a wonderfully open forum for communication and personal and family growth. The family begins to work together for the common good. Children begin to communicate with their parents in meaningful ways. Teenagers begin to feel that they are important and worthwhile in the family. It's difficult to resist understanding and empathy for another when you have truly walked a mile in his shoes as we do in a proxy RET session.

RET and Fears or Phobias

Case Study

Tim is a 30 year old man who came for RET because he was afraid to ride in airplanes, elevators, or to go across a bridge. He felt as if he would fall. He also felt closed-in and had a great need to get out or away. The older he got the more his fears seemed to grow. This phobia was seriously interfering with his personal and business life. He would feel intense fear and dread, anxiety, and physical symptoms including neck and shoulder pain, sweating, and heart palpitations. He would often hear voices when in his anxiety condition: "Watch it, he'll fall". He felt like this patterned his whole life.

In RET, Tim was able to quickly relieve the phobic symptoms and begin to make the connections between the cause and the effect of what he called "his phobia". Soon, he found himself able to release the dread and the intense fear. His physical ailments began to subside and his eyesight began to improve. The key to his case was in the phrase, "Watch it, he'll fall."

That phrase, it proved, was frozen into his bodymind at birth where the birth trauma was accompanied by a trigger

151

statement made by the attending physician when the nurse nearly dropped the newborn, Tim. This statement, associated as it was with his physical survival, had caused Tim to live a life of fearful anticipation of losing his sight ("Watch it!") and an intense fear of falling (". . .he'll fall!").

Tim has overcome the phobic symptoms, including the anxiety, sweating, neck and shoulder pains. He was very excited about RET because he was able to process his fears so rapidly that he was able to avoid the panic he usually felt when triggered into what he called his phobia. The sessions left him feeling safe and now Tim reports he has never felt better. He rides elevators and has had his first airplane ride without feeling any of the previous symptoms.

RET is particularly suited to the job of relieving the symptoms (by relieving the cause) of fears and phobias. Any traumatic emotion can be released with RET. Many clients wonder if RET is really working because they expected it to be a painful experience. They expected the "cure" would be as painful as the traumatic memories had been.

Men often comment that the session seemed uneventful, yet they felt terrific afterwards! Because volumes of emotional traumal can be addressed so quickly with RET, some clients are amazed that it doesn't have to "hurt" in order to be working!

Case Study

Stephen came in for RET because "his wife was tired of witnessing his intense fear of heights". He insisted he was justifiably afraid of heights and that his wife was overly sensitive. He felt the issue was her problem, not his. Stephen was very resistant but agreed to go througha session.

The first session was spent in an attempt to build rapport but he flatly refused to cooperate in the process.

Before his second session, his wife came in to do proxy for him. Stephen agreed to come in for a second session.

Afterward, Stephen said he would not return because he never felt a thing and didn't believe RET would do any good. Stephen's wife, however, related to us that he was now able to climb stairs and stand on ladders. He had even gone to the top floor of an apartment building to look at TV sets!

Clearly, Stephen's fear of heights had been resolved, regardless of what he said to the contrary.

Our Mission and Purpose

Many therapists who have come to train with us have caught our vision to train as many therapists as we can to handle the growing need to relieve pain and teach unconditional love and acceptance of self. Our vision is to assist in healing Mother Earth and create a new paradigm of joy.

In the next few years we will see wellness centers all over the world with healers working together as it all works together.

The Movement Toward Unconditional Love

The whole thrust of RET and the Seven Principles of Growth is the development and sharing of unconditional love. Each month we offer to our technicians a special support group for technicians where we practice the newest techniques in RET. These special sessions for technicians also allow the technicians to relieve themselves of much of the negativity they deal with during the month with their clients. We offer the opportunity to serve each other in an atmosphere of love and acceptance. The objectives again are unconditional love and light.

Occasionally, it is enjoyable for us technicians to get together and savor each other's company. Once a year we get together for a RET retreat. We love the beach for these retreats and have enjoyed many such retreats over the years. We've done all the things most people do at such occasions: we act silly with one another and have fun, fun, fun. Our RET family has spread out over the face of the earth in such a manner as to be pretty far flung. Our retreats draw in people from all over the US., Canada, Europe, China, Australia, New Zealand, and other places. What a delight for us to see the healing influence of RET in so many places around the globe.

It is our desire to awaken the planet and its inhabitants to their true selves: the light within. The negative perceptions are beginning to release and the light of love is shining through. We hope to share a vision of world peace that is awakening in the clients served by our group of technicians worldwide. The light of love is beginning to awaken in the eyes of these wonderful people, our clients. In response to the destruction so markedly displayed by the media to those who are willing to accept it, we offer an alternative view; one of awakening love and warmth; one of hope and faith; one of acceptance and inner strength. The world, rather than dying, is beginning to awaken to life. It is our desire to assist in this great awakening.

Our RET technicians discover after a short tenure of practice that the negative emotional elements and traumatic memories of their clients are so similar to their own that the awareness of generic material becomes obvious. That is, they discover that our human family has generic emotional material. We may create immensely interesting methods to assist us to experience those generic feelings, yet they are, nevertheless the same feelings that every other human being has felt at some time to some degree. Thus, we have found the generic nature of human emotions. This generic nature allows us to contact and release large amounts of emotional material in short periods of time.

Because of the "one song", the RET technician really does know how the client feels, offers empathy (a true desire to learn and understand), and through the process of proxy assists the client to let go and trust the universe. This ability to come from the point of light is imperative in the process of RET.

After technicians deal with the majority of their own issues and attended some Life Skills classes to learn about the Seven Principles, they may begin to become aware that they are becoming the light. They notice they no longer must come from the light with their clients; they are the light. The light becomes a constant companion, an escort, a creation within. Becoming the light is a major breakthrough in conscious awareness and must be experienced to be understood.

With the awareness of a being of light, the awakened person, technician or client, begins to become aware of the now, the precious present. When the clouds of the past have dispelled and the future is trusted completely, the now becomes a wondrous place to live fully. It is the ability to live fully in the now that brings about the new point of Self Awareness. With Self Awareness comes the glimpse into the realm of the objective, or God realm. Many are quite satisfied with their lives as they are without the pain of traumatic memories. Yet there are those who desire to transcend when the fetters are released. They want to soar into the stratosphere and beyond. They desire to discover what is beyond human understanding. It is there and you can find it if you want it.

The story is told of the wise old man who lived in a far away land near a lake in the tops of the mountains. His wisdom was well known among the people of the land. One day, a young man desiring light and understanding traveled up the mountains to visit the wise man. When the young man arrived at his destination he found the old man was absent from his home. He began to search for the man and finally found him at the shore of the lake. "Teach me to be wise like you." said the young man to the wise man. "Come with me out into the water," said the wise old man, and the young man followed him out into the midst of the lake. There they stood waist deep in water far from the shore.

"Get down under the water," demanded the old man. And the young man obeyed, holding his breath and ducking down into the water. The old man then held the young man under the water until he nearly drowned. When the old man let the young man up out of the water he said to him, "Young man, when you seek wisdom like you sought air, come see me."

After a program of RET and principles classes, many people feel the passion to seek further light and understanding. They become like Jonathan Seagull: wanting more from life than scraps and meagerness. The answers are there for you when you seek them. When the darkness is gone only light exists. When the light is there the darkness is gone.

The ultimate purpose of this Self Discovery Process of RET and Principles is the awakening to our native unconditional love. It is our nature to be loving. Indeed, we are expressing that love at every moment. Each of us is expressing our love for each other in the best way we know how at the time. We do so under the influence of our own traumatic memories and the collective traumas of our human consciousness. With RET, the trauma is released, freed, reframed into light and love. It is the light and love that heals.

We have awakened to a new sense of gratitude. We have so much to be grateful for. Everyday has become a delight of awareness. The joy of learning and growing has become such a fulfilling experience for us. Many of us are joining in a wonderful journey of exploration and discovery.

The feeling of gratitude is awakening in us fully.

We find that we are becoming alive in love. It is a new point of light and awareness. As the clouds are dispelling the sun is coming out and warming our hearts. We are beginning to bask in the sunlight of divine love. The journey is becoming warm and wonderful, sweet and sublime, transcendent and illuminating.

We leave you with this message that we read at the conclusion of our training sessions. It is a call to awakening the Children of the Light, which are all of us.

Children of the Light

The time of the Great Awakening is come. You who have chosen to lift our eyes from darkness to the light are blessed to see the advent of a new day on Planet Earth. Because your heart has yearned to see real peace where war has reigned, to show mercy where cruelty has dominated, and to know love where fear has frozen hearts, you are privileged to usher real healing to your world.

The Planet Earth is a blessing to you. She is your friend and your mother. Always remember and honor your relationship with her. She is a living, loving, breathing being, like unto yourself. She feels the love that you give as you walk upon her soil with a happy heart.

The Creator has chosen your hands to reach the lonely, your eyes to see innocence in the guilty, and your lips to utter words of comfort. Let pain be no more! You have wandered in dark dreams for too long now. You must step into the light and send for what you know is true. The world has suffered not from evil, but from the fear of the acknowledgment of good. That fear must be ended now, forever, and it is within your power to do so.

No one can find yourself but you. All of your answers are within. You must now teach the lessons you have learned. Your understanding has been given not only for yourself, but to guide a sore and tired world to a place of rest in a new consciousness.

Here before you is your vision come true. Here is your answer given you, a song to soothe a weary soul and make it new again. Here is the bridge that joins you to your brothers and sisters. Here is your Self. Look gently upon your self, and allow yourself to be filled by the light you have been seeing. True love comes from yourself, and every thought is a blessing to the entire universe.

All areas of your life will be healed. You will shine with a golden splendor that speaks of the One who created you in wisdom and glory. The past will dissolve like a dark dream, and your joy will be so brilliant that you will have no recollection of the night.

Go forth, and be a messenger of hope. Point the way to healing by walking in gratefulness. Your brothers and sisters will follow, and as you pass beyond the portal of limitation, you will be united and reunited with all who seem to be lost. There is no loss in the Creator. Choose the path of forgiveness, and you will weep tears of joy for the goodness you find in all.

Go forth and live the life of the radiant soul that you are. Glorify the Creator in your every deed. You are important; you are needed, and you are worthy. Neither allow the dark cloak of fear to hide the light from your view.

You were not born to fail; you are destined to succeed. The hope of the world has been planted in your breast, and you are assured of success as you stand for the One who Created you.

This then is the healing of Planet Earth. All of your doubts and fears can be set aside as you know that the healing will come through the love in your heart.

—Author unknown

Conclusion

Controlled research continues by leading professionals in the fields of neurology and clinical psychology through grants on the east coast as well as here on the west coast.

We are dedicated to the continued and ongoing expansion of Rapid Eye Technology and our vision to facilitate the healing of the earth on the physical, emotional, mental and spiritual planes.

Namasté.
The light and love in me honors the light and love in you!

Ranae

Testimonials

Thank you for Rapid Eye Therapy. It has changed my life, I now have let go of fear and stress. My health, mental, emotional and physical has improved so much. Keep up the good work! H.L.

The love and encouragement given to me at The Center assisted my healing as much as RET. I'm so thankful that everyone taking the training for RET must first do their own work. I never dreamed how much better I would feel. M.G. (RET Therapist)

It is directly due to RET that I feel ready and able to move forward in spiritual work! E.T.

Thank you for the courage it took to listen to the Spirit and for the work you are doing. I can't believe how it has changed my life. I can't wait until I can help others! S.H.

I prayed for help, the doors were opened and I appreciate you and the growth in me that RET has facilitated. K. G.

Only someone who has experienced a true release could appreciate how RET has released me from bondage! Understanding just keeps coming to me! A.S.

Each day I live now is so new and fulfilling! It's so wo____
people heal and grow. Thanks for RET and the Severe _____
changes lives, I hope you feel the love I radiate towards _____

A Miracle! I'm communicating with my family. Th____
for RFT and proxy work. Thank you for training my ther a____
talking again! J.B

Your flow of wisdom has encouraged me to go within and acknow___
my own wisdom and worth. Namasté W.B.

My beautiful sister of light, I will never forget my therapy and
training. I am so grateful, my life has changed. I have come from
being suicidal to Bliss. You are the BEST! K.K

Because of RET I have let go of my own abuse after years of pain and
a broken marriage. I feel whole and healed. I can only repay this by
taking the training and helping others trapped in pain. I. T

I have a record of abusing and have served time in jail. After a year
of RET and cognitive class work, I felt I could be on my own. It's been
two years now since I last felt the compulsion to abuse. I still have a
session once in a while to maintain strength. I am eternally grateful for
RET. It's a miracle in my life. A.J.

Thanks to RET, my arm is recovered enough to get off disability.
When I forgave and released the abuse from my father, my arm
healed. You should see me swing my hammer now! J.O.